I WASN'T RAISED  TO PLAY BY THEIR RULES

VMH™ Publishing

ALSO BY THIS AUTHOR:

Straight Out of Hell 1- Wrong Place, Wrong Time

Straight Out of Hell 2 - The True Character of a Man

I WASN'T RAISED TO PLAY BY THEIR RULES

GARRY L. JONES

VMH™ Publishing

The publisher is not responsible for websites, or social media pages (or their content) related to this publication, that are not owned by the publisher. Quantity sales. Special discounts are available on quantity purchases by corporations, associations, and others. For details, contact the publisher.

Paperback ISBN: 979-8-9918361-8-0

Hardback ISBN: 979-8-9918361-9-7

Author's Note:

The names and characters have been changed to protect the privacy of such individual's. The events documented in this publication are according to the author's memory.

Published in United States of America

10 9 8 7 6 5 4 3 2 1

This book is dedicated to Mrs. Tessie Jones

The Source of Your Strength

It's been three hundred and sixty five days since
we put you to rest.
The strength you instilled in your family is still
being put to the test.
Some of the same people who attended your home going
celebration last year are no longer here, but their spirits have
departed their body and they are somewhere near.

The Source of Your Strength

There are still times when we go through our
moments of despair,
But it's getting easier to wake up and realize
you are no longer there.
The source of your strength has carried us a long ways, And
because of your strength we can handle the difficult days.

The Source of Your Strength

Some families grow apart when the matriarch dies,
If someone says anything different about us, I will have to say
they are telling lies.
We have come together to support each other's affliction,
diseases, and pain.
Thanks to you to the source of your strength has done it again.
The Jones' and the Simmons are not set apart, the fire still
continues to burn,
And we will carry the torch and run.

The Source of Your Strength

One of the hardest things we had to do on the one-year
anniversary of your death is bury your great nephew.
The family came together and did what we had to do because of
the love we have for you.
We visited your gravesite as well as your sister and son, We
didn't cry, as a matter of fact we had fun.
If it weren't for your strength you instilled in us our light would
no longer burn.

TABLE OF CONTENTS

CHAPTER 1

New Warden, Same Captain: EEO Complaint P-99-0116

If you haven't picked up my other two books, *Straight Out of Hell One: Wrong Place Wrong Time* and *Straight Out of Hell 2: The True Character of a Man,* I'd advise you to do so. The second book ended with the 'food strike' at the Federal Correctional Institution in Tallahassee, Fla.

I was working for a feeble-minded captain. My health had started to decline under my last captain. I explained to my new captain that I was suffering from chest pains; I'd been on the 4 p.m. to midnight shift for 16 months at the Federal Correctional Institution. Lieutenants are supposed to shift every quarter to avoid burnout.

One white lieutenant was suffering from the same chest pains and anxiety attacks I was coping with; he'd worked the same shift, but only for three months. When he put in a request to be assigned to the Federal Detention Center for medical reasons, his request was granted. The Federal Detention Center (FDC) is laid back, and lieutenants didn't have to do much work because the facility was a control movement-type of detention center, meaning all the inmates were locked down and couldn't exit their cells unless let out by a staff member. The FDC housed men only, while the FCI housed women inmates. When I arrived in Tallahassee, both the FCI and FDC housed male inmates.

By 1996, the FCI had been converted to a female institution. Working with female inmates is totally different from working with males—day and night. The women constantly bitched and complained about problems, all day and night, and never accepted «no» for an answer. Then I had to go home and hear the same shit. I couldn't catch a break. Some women—not all— would have nagged the hell out of Satan. The lieutenants at the Federal Correctional Institution (FCI) had to maintain the roster for the FDC and FCI. If someone called in sick, they had to ensure both institutions had proper coverage. For example, if an inmate got sick and needed to go to the hospital, the FCI lieutenant had to find a staff member to ride in the ambulance for both institutions, and then find someone to take the place of the staff member riding in the ambulance.

They also had to find staff members to work overtime. Officers were calling in sick all the time. If you were sick, you were supposed to notify the shift lieutenant two hours in advance so your supervisor could find someone to pick up the overtime. Most officers called in sick five minutes before the shift started, putting a lot of pressure on the lieutenants to replace that officer.

By policy, there was supposed to be a senior lieutenant and an activities lieutenant to run each shift. The activities lieutenant worked under the shift lieutenant—that's how they were ranked. As it turned out, I didn't have an activities lieutenant to assist me on my shift ninety-nine percent of the time. That's why I got burned out so easily—the captain purposely made sure my shift was short-staffed.

When you're short-staffed trying to run a prison, mistakes get made. When mistakes are made, the captain doesn't want to hear that you were short-staffed—this only applied to me. Only by the grace of God were very few mistakes made on these shifts. But I started experiencing severe chest pains, and when I went to the doctor, I was told that I had aorta inefficiency; when I'm under a lot of stress, the pain kicks in.

I had been having these pains for months, but I dismissed them, assuming I had strained a muscle while working out. Several times, I left work to go to the emergency room for these chest pains. When I explained to the captain that the doctor stated I needed to be assigned to a low-stress environment, she gave me the attitude that she didn't give a damn. I told her I wanted to be afforded the same opportunity that the white lieutenant had when he complained about chest pains, and his doctor recommended he be put at the Federal Detention Center, where the stress for lieutenants was very low. After I complained, the captain kept me working at the Federal Correctional Institution and put me on the midnight to 8 a.m. shift. She claimed this shift was less stressful, and normally it is—assuming you had medical staff working to administer medical care for the inmates if they got sick in the middle of the night.

But the Bureau of Prisons was cutting back on its budget to save money, and they eliminated medical staff from working the midnight shift—which put plenty of stress on the lieutenant when inmates got sick with heart attacks and all kinds of problems. Lieutenants and officers are trained in CPR, but that's the only medical training we had. The outside world probably thinks the only thing you have to do is call an ambulance if an inmate gets sick, but it's not that easy. You had to call the medical staff at home and inform them of the sick inmates, and their job was to come in and treat the inmate—except that never happened.

This made things worse for lieutenants. The medical staff would claim the inmate didn't need to go to the hospital; but as the lieutenant, you're watching the inmate's eyes roll back in their head, their skin color changing, and some inmates bent over coughing up blood. I'd call the Control Center and tell them to dispatch an ambulance to the institution—I didn't give a damn what the medical staff was saying on the phone. The only thing I knew was what I saw in front of my own eyes: an inmate dying.

I had to find two staff members to ride with the inmate to the hospital, and we were already short-staffed. But that didn't matter, even though I knew I'd get chewed out for making that decision when the medical staff was making the exact opposite recommendation. I had a decision to make: either let the inmate die or live. The medical staff knew they were required to return to the institution to assess the inmate, but they were too lazy to get out of bed. Instead, they'd say, "The inmate is all right; I'll see them at sick call in the morning."

The Bureau of Prisons was always finding ways to cut its budget, even at the risk of putting human lives in jeopardy. It's hard to put all the blame on BOP because the inmates knew we didn't have medical staff available on the midnight shift and would start complaining of chest pains right after midnight. I knew some of them were faking, but that's a chance you can't take. I've seen inmates have a heart attack and die right in front of me; if they insist their chest hurts, better safe than sorry. We weren't trained in taking EKGs—in fact, some of the medical staff didn't know how to operate one, either. Some of our medical workers hadn't been able to land a medical job in the private sector, and some didn't know a damn thing about treating patients.

Now you can see why I was stressed out and desired a transfer to the FDC. The lieutenant at the FDC didn't have to do a damn thing except make rounds and ensure the key count was done. It was unfortunate I had to file an EEO (Equal Employment Opportunity) complaint, but I had to in order to stop her madness.

After I filed the complaint, BOP (Bureau of Prisons) started retaliating against me. I'm not naïve; I knew this could happen when I filed it. Shortly afterward, the warden retired and, ironically, became the warden of the DC Department of Correction in Lorton. I knew he wasn't going to last long in D.C.

The warden did everything he could to destroy me, but he didn't last a whole year at Lorton. The new warden who came to Tallahassee decided to clean house, and it was obvious my EEO complaints were taking a toll on Tallahassee, even though after the investigation report was returned to me, the EEO office decided my complaints didn't have any merit.

The Bureau of Prisons will do everything they can to make it appear your complaints are frivolous. When the new warden arrived, the captain's career started to fade. The captain's disciplinary reports on me weren't sticking; the warden could see that I was being targeted. When I received my annual evaluation, my captain downgraded it to "exceed" when it should have been an "outstanding." When I sent this information to the warden, she asked if I could prove I deserved an outstanding evaluation. I told her to give me a day, and I would send her a report of everything I did that the captain didn't include in my evaluation. After the warden read my evidence, she upgraded my evaluation to outstanding, and the captain received a satisfactory evaluation for trying to undermine my performance.

As a matter of fact, the captain's yearly evaluation had consequences. Soon after the captain received her evaluation, I got word that she was being demoted to unit manager and sent to another institution. When she got demoted, she was still able to keep her current salary. I might add that Correctional Services is the biggest department in the Federal Bureau of Prisons, and the captain is responsible for all security matters—as well as being required to supervise the staff. When you go from captain to unit manager, it demonstrates you're not able to supervise a large department, even though both are GS-12 positions. The unit manager only supervises a couple of staff members.

CHAPTER 2

The Retaliation Continues In My Home

When you file an EEO complaint, retaliation comes from every angle. When I moved to Tallahassee, I got government housing that cost $670 a month, with electricity included—and the government was your landlord. Before the new warden arrived, I'd been having trouble getting the government to stop flooding in my basement. Every time it rained, the basement would flood. My oldest son, Derrick, was staying down there, and the government took their time looking into the problem.

I believe that because I had filed an EEO complaint, the institution guaranteed that my flooding problem was a low priority. I didn't give a damn about how the BOP (Bureau of Prisons) treated me, but my family had nothing to do with this.

I had to file another EEO complaint about my living conditions. My complaint read as follows:

"My name is Garry Jones. I am a Lieutenant at the Federal Correctional Institution in Tallahassee, Florida. At present, I am housed in staff housing. I am registering complaints of unfair housing, discrimination regarding housing, retaliation, and malice. On several occasions, I have contacted both Chief of Mechanical Services, Jimmy Wheeler, and associates Wardens Reese Marvin, Candice Mack, and Rosber Daniels, as well as Warden Mary Smith, about suitable and equitable housing in the staff residential housing, but to no avail.

From September 14, 1998, to October 29, 1999, I made numerous requests and notifications to the above-listed persons to provide my family and me with suitable and equitable living conditions. I have been in staff housing since August 1995. I had all the living accommodations I needed when my family and I moved into staff housing in August 1995. During the latter part of 1996, hard rains came; the basement began to leak, subsequently causing it to flood and resulting in property damage. The basement smelled of sour odors (sewage) throughout the house. This was to the point that all the carpet had to be removed from the basement and was not replaced. The windows and doors had to be opened to breathe and ventilate the house. My family and I were stuck with the cleanup of this mess. On several occasions, private plumbing firms were called out to alleviate the problems, but to no avail. As a result, my family and I have been subjected to unsuitable living conditions due to the flooding, the smells of sour odor, and the basement not being accessible for storage or recreation with my children."

While this was going on, Rosber Daniels, the associate warden, approached me and told me I should move into the community or wait eight months until the house could be repaired. Mind you, this was never suggested to the other tenants. This meant I'd have to pay out of my own pocket to uproot my family and find another home at my own expense. This was done as a means of retaliation, discrimination, and malice due to my notifications to the warden about my problems with staff housing. It's my belief that Daniels was responsible for the delay in getting suitable living space because I was interviewed by investigators during a previous grievance filing by another applicant regarding staff housing. From that day forward, I will always believe he had malice in his heart and was discriminating against me and my family. For that reason, it's not only illegal; it's personal.

Again, I contacted Warden Smith about the housing situation. Before getting a response, my basement flooded again, with water seeping through the walls and the smell of sewage flowing throughout the house. I called Warden Smith, who also lived in staff housing, and asked her to come to my house to see the problems firsthand. After visiting the home, she asked if I had a problem moving into the vacant staff house next door. I agreed to do that.

First, we had to wait for the facilities department to complete the touch-up work in the house. We started moving in May 1999; the house was supposed to have all the necessary accommodations, including a basement, two full bedrooms, a bathroom, and a family room. To our dismay, the basement had been gutted. The ceiling and walls were removed, electrical wiring was exposed and hanging from the ceiling. I suspect Daniels instructed the chief of mechanical services, Jimmy Wheeler, and his staff to rip the walls and ceilings from the basement of that house—again, done as a means of retaliation, malice, and discrimination. Everyone else residing in staff housing had accessible basements, and the necessary repairs and renovations in their homes were completed without delay. I was charged the same amount for housing as everyone else, but I didn't have the same accommodations.

Needless to say, they never fixed the basement, and the retaliation continued. Later, I found out through one of the staff members that the first house I moved into was full of lead-based paint. I filed a complaint with the institution and the Occupational Safety and Health Administration, and to my surprise, the federal agency said that wasn't a problem they handled and closed my case.

CHAPTER 3

The New Warden Only Worked One Year Because of the Corruption

There was so much corruption at the Federal Correctional Institution that the warden didn't last a year. Before Warden Smith left, she stopped by my office one day and said, "Lieutenant Jones, I ordered the investigation against you to be dropped."

I asked her which investigation she was talking about. "The investigation about you and Officer Linda Fike having an affair," she replied. "When you're a lieutenant, you can't have an affair with your subordinate, and as long as that investigation continues, you cannot be promoted."

After telling me the investigation didn't have any merit, Warden Smith tried to convince me to accept a captain position at another institution. I told her no; I was staying in Tallahassee until my daughter graduated.

After the captain left, his replacement picked up right where the former captain left off—trying to destroy me. Even though the previous captain had been demoted, someone higher up still didn't like what had happened to her, but they didn't have a choice but to demote her. Despite my EEO complaint being deemed without merit, I didn't stop there. I filed a lawsuit against the former captain.

The BOP wasn't finished with me. The new captain arrived and held a meeting for the lieutenants, stating he came to this institution to get rid of three lieutenants. I assumed he was talking about Walkerfountaine, Caldwell, and me. While he didn't clearly name who he wanted out, I already knew who he was targeting. I even asked him if I was one of them, and he didn't joke about it—he said yes. He warned that if I didn't complete my paperwork on time, I'd be the first lieutenant he got rid of.

This captain didn't realize I knew more about his position than he did. The fact is, all three lieutenants he was targeting had been following policy and procedures, but the BOP still wanted to get rid of us. We all had EEO complaints against the BOP, and we couldn't understand why we were getting this kind of treatment when we were trying to do the right thing. Before the new captain arrived, I had started seeing a psychiatrist because my physical health was declining, and now my mental health was suffering as well. Every day I came to work, I had to pray in the parking lot for the Lord's protection because the BOP administration was coming after me. The only reason I lasted this long was my faith in God and the fact that I was a warrior myself.

It wasn't in my nature to let anyone walk all over me and get away with it. But I was on the verge of losing my mind because of the relentless retaliation. The government has so much damn bureaucracy that you can't even do the work you were hired to do.

CHAPTER 4

Another Warden Reports to the Institution

The new warden was different in more ways than one. Standing at about 5'3", she loved to wear high heels and seemed determined to strut around the facility like a queen. It wasn't unusual to see the warden at a club, partying it up. While what she did was her business, inmates started to talk about her frequency at these establishments and how often she got drunk. Staff would spot her at the club and return to report it to the inmates. This warden didn't give a damn about our procedures and knew nothing about policy.

The BOP organization was out to get anyone who exposed its unfair treatment of both staff and inmates. My captain had already made it clear he was gunning for me and a couple of my buddies. For someone to come in and make a blanket statement like, "I came to get rid of you," was a strong indication that they always had someone within BOP who would protect them. We often referred to this as a Bureau Daddy or Bureau Mom—anyone from a warden, regional director, or director of the BOP, all the way to anyone with power. In truth, these "moms" and "dads" acted like mentors. When the new captain started, it felt like déjà vu all over again.

My supervisors believed they had someone in their corner and could act with impunity, knowing they could get away with it through a phone call to the right person. Instead of making the institution proud, they often infuriated their mentors, who risked their jobs to protect them whenever trouble arose. My own mentor had a Bureau Daddy, and I often wished I could find out who was backing him so I could expose them. Some people just can't handle power or a position of authority. As a lieutenant, I made it a point not to let power go to my head.

Mr. Flowers was my mentor, and I did everything within my power not to embarrass him. I learned all the policies and procedures and made sure I treated everyone with respect, whether they were an officer or an inmate. It was tough for me to respect someone who didn't show me the same courtesy. Usually, I took the high road when staff members under my supervision made errors; I wasn't eager to hand out disciplinary actions. I preferred to counsel them and offer second chances. I'm not saying I didn't take disciplinary action when necessary; I did. My mindset was that if I could save a staff member or help them keep their job—regardless of their race—I would do so.

When the new warden arrived in Tallahassee, she went to personnel and decided to cut back on staff members receiving awards. Usually, when someone received an award, they also received a monetary bonus. The BOP was looking for ways to save money, so they implemented a hiring freeze and slashed overtime. The result was burnout among staff, as we had to work with fewer people. During my shift, I was usually given the bare minimum of staff; most often, this was done intentionally.

The 4 p.m. to midnight shift was when all the illegal activities would take place. I was supposed to have an activities lieutenant working under me, but like I said earlier, 99 percent of the time, I didn't have anyone to run my shift. The activities lieutenant's job was to monitor everything that took place in the institution, including overseeing inmate meals, recreation, and church activities. The GS-11 lieutenant (Senior Lieutenant) was responsible for the overall operations of the institution, especially the paperwork. While I could run the shift myself, I knew I would eventually burn out. It was impossible to manage an institution without any help. Every day, inmates got sick, and I had to find someone to ride in the ambulance with them. The stress was mounting, and I had to pull staff from other departments to ensure they had escort training.

When an inmate's life was in danger, we often had to do whatever was necessary to get them medical care and deal with consequences later. Transporting an inmate to the hospital involved a mountain of paperwork and making sure the proper staff with escort training was assigned. Some situations required armed escorts to ensure public safety. The captain had to be notified, as well as the associate warden, warden, and duty officer. Some days, two or three inmates would need to be taken to the local hospital, and I'd be scrambling to find help while the captain just sat back, waiting for me to make an error on the paperwork.

He had already warned me that he was going to dump a shitload of paperwork on me, and he kept that promise. I was already stressed out over what the previous captain had put me through, and now this new captain was sent to finish me off. I was seeing a psychiatrist for stress and depression, had marital problems, and at work, I felt trapped. I dreaded coming home and hated going to work. I couldn't tell which one was worse.

I often came home and sat in my car, drinking because I didn't want to go inside. When I got to work, I had to read a scripture before stepping inside the institution, asking God to be with me because I knew it was only a matter of time before I snapped and hurt someone. My doctor frequently suggested I retire, but retirement wasn't the answer; I was a warrior at heart. He warned me that if I continued to endure these changes at work and at home, I'd eventually have a nervous breakdown. He said if it weren't for treating others in the same job, he wouldn't believe a word I was saying.

In April 2000, we received a memo from the captain stating we needed to complete our quarterly evaluations and the yearly evaluation for the officers. In his memo, the captain insisted these had to be finished within two weeks. I had nine officers to evaluate. In order to determine the officers' yearly evaluations, lieutenants had to sum up the evaluations from all three quarters. Officers were graded as minimum successful, fully successful, exceeds, or outstanding. Just because one lieutenant wrote an officer's yearly evaluation doesn't mean that same lieutenant also completed their quarterly evaluations throughout the year, since officers work under different lieutenants at various times.

I calculated the officers' quarterly evaluations and assigned them a rating for the year. Each officer was rated in five categories, four times a year. Before I had my first encounter with the captain, I remember visiting my doctor at 2 p.m. My shift started at 4 p.m., and my doctor asked how everything was going at work. I told him I was catching hell and didn't know how much longer I could take it. He suggested I take some time off before things escalated, but I didn't want time off. The real issue was that the captain was overloading me with paperwork, and I had to ensure everything was perfect. If I made a mistake, I was facing counseling or other extreme disciplinary actions.

I pointed out to my doctor that other lieutenants had the proper staff to work their shifts, while I didn't. Mistakes made by other lieutenants often went unnoticed, but if I made one—even if those errors were few and far between—I had to prove it wasn't a mistake. Most captains I worked for didn't know shit about policy and procedures, and neither did the wardens, which made everything even more frustrating. Most of the time, disciplinary actions against me went through the associate warden and warden as well. I would have to research our regulations and guidelines to demonstrate I hadn't made an error.

More often than not, actions taken against me were dismissed after I exposed the administration's ignorance of their own policies and procedures. I was getting burned out trying to prove to the administration what they should have already known. Working for these feeble-minded people who were hell-bent on taking me down was clearly taking a toll on my health.

CHAPTER 5

Snapped

"Lieutenant Jones, I need to see you in my office," the captain told me right after I had started my shift. From the tone of his voice, I knew he'd already figured out another way to undermine my authority.

I asked a fellow lieutenant to accompany me to the captain's office because I wanted a witness. The captain was determined to make me bow down to him; he knows how to instill fear in other lieutenants' hearts, but mine had become as hard and cold as his.

"I thought I told you to downgrade evaluations," he said, then looked up, noticed who was with me, and added, "Why is Lieutenant Walkerfountaine in the office? She needs to leave."

I turned to her and asked Walkerfountaine to stay. It was in my best interest to have a witness, and frankly, it was good for the captain too, considering I wanted to beat the hell out of him.

"Captain, I didn't spend all that time working on the officers' evaluations just to turn around and downgrade them. I gave them exactly what they deserved based on their performances this quarter," I responded. The conversation got tense.

"Lieutenant Jones, change the evaluations."

"No, captain, I'm not changing them."

"Well, Lieutenant Jones, if you don't downgrade the evaluations, I'm going to bring disciplinary action against you."

I refused to back down.

"Captain, I don't give a damn about your disciplinary action against me," I shot back. "It will be a cold day in hell before I change anything. Furthermore, you need to read your own policy. It states that if the captain disagrees with the lieutenant's evaluations of the officers, then he has the authority to change the lieutenant's evaluations.

"Now," I added, "go by policy and do your job. Captain, you change the evaluations."

At first, neither of us backed down.

"Lieutenant Jones, you must be afraid of what the officers are going to say if you change their evaluation," the captain said.

"Don't give me that bullshit reverse psychology crap," I shot back. "I'm a man, and when a man gives you his word that he isn't going to do something, he means it, and I'm that man. Why aren't you calling for the rest of the lieutenants to change their evaluations? Is it because all the performance evaluations I have are for black officers and you want to make sure that the white officers get their outstanding evaluations to secure their monetary yearly awards?"

That was it. I left the captain's office and returned to mine to run my shift. A few minutes later, the captain came back to my office and said, "Lieutenant Jones, you need to change these evaluations."

I could feel myself losing it.

"Look, jackass, I'm not changing a damn thing."

The captain stormed out, and I sat down to call my doctor. I told him I was about to kill this guy if I didn't leave work immediately—my doctor ordered me to do just that.

I returned to the captain and told him my doctor wanted me to come see him right away, but the captain refused to release me.

"What's your doctor's name and number, Lieutenant Jones, and why does he want you to leave the institution?" he asked.

"When you call, he's not going to discuss my medical issues. If you don't allow me to leave, I'm going to pick your narrow white ass up and throw you through that damn window. Now get me a relief before I break your neck."

When I said that, the captain turned red and started trembling. I called a friend to pick me up and later went to see my doctor.

"Garry, you need some rest, and I'm going to give you two weeks off," my doctor told me. "Maybe you can go visit some family members." This was just what I needed.

I arranged to fly to Washington, D.C., because I couldn't go back home. My wife was behaving as badly as the captain, nagging the hell out of me and at one point telling me, "You need to leave those white people alone. It's not about black and white; it's about right and wrong." When I came home from work and my wife was there, I would either get in my bed or sit in the garage drinking. I was doubling up on my medication, trying to cope with hell at work and misery at home.

When I got to D.C., I stayed with a friend who let me chill. He didn't drink at all, but I did to calm my nerves. After visiting everyone I knew in Washington, I returned to Tallahassee. But as soon as my plane landed, I began to feel sick. Partly because I knew I had to go back to work and face the captain.

No surprise—right when I got back, the captain picked up right where he'd left off. He had changed my post to work activities lieutenant, which was illegal since I was a senior and not a junior lieutenant. The warden allowed him to get away with it, though. I asked why my post had changed, and the captain stated he could do whatever he wanted.

He had figured out a way to retaliate against me. I worked the post for a week and filed an EEO complaint, prompting the warden to put me back in my old post. She knew the captain had been wrong to demote me, but she didn't care. The fact that the warden didn't understand her own institution's policies allowed the captain to run circles around her. All he had to do was send the paperwork to her, and she would sign it before even bothering to read it—but that's what ended up biting her in the ass this time. I had to put that paperwork in their faces in order for them to back off, but the administrative echelon was all in cahoots, from the regional director to the director of the Federal Bureau of Prisons. The EEO division was a joke; they ensured that any complaints filed would come back marked "without merit." Normally when you filed an EEO complaint, the division was supposed to investigate it within 180 days. When I filed EEO complaints, it took at least two years for them to complete their investigations. But if I missed the deadline for my complaint, I couldn't get an extension, and it was automatically dismissed.

The Tactic My EEO Counselor Used

At this point, the institution came at me like I was a terrorist; they were determined to destroy me once and for all. I don't mind being a team player, but only if the team plays by the rules and regulations already in place. Sometimes I think the fact that I wasn't dying drove the institution crazy. Whenever the U.S. goes to war, they use air assaults to break the enemy down; but those enemies just keep rising up again. Even though the U.S. doesn't like using ground troops to fight guerrilla warfare, sometimes they have no choice. We've been in Iraq for more than a decade now and still can't crush the enemy. Now we have to depart with our heads between our legs, thousands of troops dead, and trillions of dollars spent on an unnecessary war.

In a similar spirit, every time I filed an EEO complaint, the administration hit back with full force. Only God gave me the strength to endure it. It wasn't easy, and I shed more tears and had more sleepless nights than I can shake a stick at.

Growing up in urban housing projects and remembering what my family taught me paid off—I wasn't going down easy. My attitude was that I would break you down before you broke me down, even if I had to lose my own life doing it. The spirit of David was in me, but the spirit of Saul was in my enemies at the institution.

One day, I contacted my EEO counselor and told her I needed to file an amendment to my complaints. I didn't trust her, though, because every time we set up a meeting, she'd skip it. That meant I was quickly running out of time to file something. This was done on purpose. She avoided meeting with me because she was in cahoots with the institution, and I couldn't file a complaint after the deadline had passed.

But this time, we did meet that afternoon. "You might as well drop this complaint because the deadline for your paperwork is today, and you aren't going to make it in time," she informed me.

I told her to fill out the paperwork and let me worry about that. I knew if I got to the Post Office before 5 p.m. and my letter was postmarked that day, it would be considered valid. So, I made it there at 4:45 and asked the postal clerk to ensure today's date was on it. He guaranteed me it would be.

EEO counselors are trained to ensure your complaints remain at the institutional level, and if they can't, they try to convince you not to file. The tactic used against me was that my EEO counselor would cancel our meetings to let the deadline lapse. But I understood their game, and I was getting just as good—if not better—at playing it. I kept myself aware of the official policies; God and policy were my weapons.

CHAPTER 7

EEO Complaint P-2000-0187

On August 14, 2000, I contacted my EEO counselor to amend my complaints, but she claimed she couldn't meet with me at that time. Speaking by phone, I told her it was the last date to file, and it wasn't my fault she kept canceling our meetings. I made it clear I'd let everyone know she had canceled our meetings to keep me from filing my complaint, which read:

"It is my contention that I have been the victim of racial discrimination, harassment, and mean-spirited indifference. Sometime during February, when Derrick Hanes, the newly selected captain at the Federal Correctional Institution (Tallahassee), was with the staff assist team, I was told by a lieutenant that Lt. Morris overheard Captain Hanes tell the staff assist team that when he reports to Tallahassee, he was going to get rid of me and three other lieutenants.

In our first lieutenants' meeting with Captain Hanes, I asked him if it was true that he made that statement about getting rid of me. He never denied it but said, "If you make it hard for me, I'm going to make it hard for you."

In March 2000, Captain Hanes called me at home to allege that I was trying to get out of making up annual training courses. Of course, I wasn't trying to dodge training; any lieutenant would have loved to be in annual training to avoid the stress of being in the institution. "If you are trying to dodge annual training, I'm going to give you a shitload of work," the captain said.

I explained the recent death of my uncle, James Simmons, and that I certainly wasn't trying to get out of anything. I had even inquired about making up the annual training and was told by Vera Kodie, the EDM assistant, that it was my problem. This was very unprofessional because everyone was in on the plot to set me up.

I couldn't fathom how he could approach the issue so unprofessionally. I even volunteered to make up training on March 22, 2000. I had no intention of dodging training. I was told by Renee Wayne, head of the EDM department, that she told the captain I tried to dodge annual training every year. She was also lying; the only time I missed annual training was back in 1996 when I had surgery, and I asked Wayne for a copy of the training schedule from 1996 to 2000. When she checked it, she found I hadn't missed annual training for any reason except to have surgery.

Lies were being spread about me in every department. Even when I proved people were lying, the institution still went against me.

Captain Hanes asked how I planned to make up the training. I told him I would have to reschedule it. Hanes insisted

I'd have to make up the training on my own time and wouldn't be compensated. Whenever someone misses training, we have to provide valid proof of why we couldn't attend, and the institution is required to reschedule that person for training—it can't require them to do it on their days off. They can reschedule their days off to fit in the missed training.

On March 22, 2000, I reported for training from 7:30 a.m. to 4 p.m., even though I had to start work at 4 o'clock that day. While I was in training, I called Lt. Morris to check if we had enough people to cover me because I wanted to leave early for my flight out of town at 6 a.m. Lt. Morris said he would send a GS-8 officer to relieve me after getting the captain's permission.

I knew what the captain was going to say; it wasn't unusual for a GS-8 officer to cover for a lieutenant at the Federal Detention Center. Captain Hanes said he wasn't going to approve my request because he didn't want any GS-8 officer working as a lieutenant at FDC. However, when I reported to work at FDC that day for the 4 p.m. to midnight shift, I relieved a GS-8 officer acting as a lieutenant on the previous shift.

It should be noted that daily rosters routinely reflect GS-8 officers working various shifts at FDC in the capacity of lieutenant. Furthermore, we received a deficiency rating in this area for continuing to allow GS-8 officers to work as lieutenants at FDC.

It's obvious that the captain's refusal to grant me annual leave was personal, displaying discrimination since GS-11 lieutenants are often granted sick and annual leave while he simply vacates his post.

On March 28, 2000, I was called into the captain's office and asked why I had chosen to use comp time when I reported to training. I informed him that I'd come to training on my own time because he refused to schedule it for me. That same day, the captain falsely alleged that I was guilty of sexual harassment during annual training. I told him he was lying and demanded a full investigation to prove these allegations were false. I wanted everyone in the training session to write a memo confirming that the instructor was lying.

I asked the training instructor if she had an opening in her department because I saw on the board that they needed someone, and I was going to apply. I immediately told the captain I wanted the warden contacted regarding these allegations, but he said that wasn't necessary because we could handle this issue at his level. I refused and contacted the warden, who said she'd have to consult the captain to find out what had transpired.

The captain claimed it was a misunderstanding, giving that excuse to the warden because he made the whole thing up. I refused to let it go. I wanted something to be done.

When I filed paperwork to dispute the instructor's claim, I later discovered her response was that she hadn't told the captain that I sexually harassed her. She stated that she didn't like me asking about the position that was open in her department and that I said I would fill out an application because I didn't want to work in Correctional Services anymore.

I told the captain that the instructor wasn't my type because I didn't sleep with white women. I don't have anything against white women—I simply never had a desire to sleep with any, and at that time, I was married.

On April 18, 2000, Captain Hanes called me to his office to quiz me about why I had evaluated certain officers the way I did. On May 8, 2000, I was on leave at the request of my physician, Dr. Bruce. This was a direct result of Captain Hanes pushing me into a corner by insisting that I had unfairly assessed other officers.

Nonetheless, I was shocked that Captain Hanes would even question my integrity. He said that after reviewing the evaluations, he found that 60 percent of the officers at the institution shouldn't receive outstanding evaluations because the lieutenants had given them good marks. He said there was nothing he could do, but beginning the next quarter, we lieutenants would have to justify giving officers outstanding ratings. I had always done that and could always justify those ratings. The last captain had even sent me a note saying, "Good job" regarding my evaluations, even though that captain was a black snake.

Captain Hanes insisted I change the evaluation, and when I stated my intent not to do that, he threatened to discipline me.

Instead of exchanging venom for venom with the captain, I called my doctor and informed him of the situation. He told me to prepare to leave the building for a consultation, but the captain kept pushing me until I snapped. I told Captain Hanes what my doctor had said, and while he asked for more information, I opted not to divulge my personal medical issues in detail. A few days later, while recuperating at home, Captain Hanes sent me an express mail envelope with a memo dated April 28, 2000.

I returned to work on May 14, which just so happened to be my daughter's birthday. The lieutenant's roster for the quarter of June 18 through September 9 was posted, detailing where each lieutenant was scheduled to work. I got the SR2 post, usually filled by lieutenants with less experience, like GS-9 lieutenants.

On June 19, the roster had me working as activities lieutenant until July 1. The next day, I was reassigned back to my GS-11 lieutenant post. This situation of being assigned to a lesser-experienced post added so much stress that my doctor put me in the hospital.

While I was there, my wife brought me a FedEx letter from the institution. When I opened it, Captain Hanes had sent me another memo asking my physician to answer eight questions about my health. Every time I had recuperated, I received a letter from Captain Hanes requesting I explain my need for sick leave. The Bureau of Prisons had been using tactics like this for years and managed to get away with it. I remember speaking to a former lieutenant who was now a unit manager. Mr. Burns informed me that when he worked at the Federal Correctional Institution in Jessup, Georgia, Captain Hanes was also a lieutenant and had experienced the same situation of being relegated to an SR-2 post while being a GS-11 lieutenant.

Mr. Burns shared that he had surgery on his eye and that Captain Cooper insisted he return to work before he was scheduled to. When Mr. Burns explained that he couldn't come back that quickly, the captain got furious. When Mr. Burns did return to work, he was placed on the SR-2 post typically occupied by GS-9 lieutenants. This highlights that when employees take sick leave for an extended period, they face harassment from their supervisors. Ironically, Captain Cooper was Captain Hanes's mentor when he was a lieutenant.

My doctor kept urging me to retire because I couldn't continue dealing with stress at work and home, but I was a fighter, and I couldn't let anyone punk me.

A lot of things were coming at me at once. Captain Hanes was out to get me but kept making mistakes and failed to cover his ass. Everyone in the institution, including the inmates, knew he was gunning for me. The harder he tried, the more I capitalized on his mistakes. The more he tried to discipline me, the faster the warden realized the two of them didn't know the policy.

The only reason the warden knew any of this is that whenever Captain Hanes disciplined me, I would research policy and send it to her—and she would order him to expunge the disciplinary action against me.

On November 17, I had to keep adding amendments to my EEO complaints. My memo stated, "Mrs. Vanessa, I would like to add these statements to my complaint. I realize I'm still being discriminated against by Captain Hanes. The latest incident occurred when Captain Hanes assigned me to work the Federal Correctional Institution on the midnight shift. Currently, I am working the midnight shift, and he has assigned me again to work the midnight shift for the next quarter. The lieutenants are supposed to rotate every quarter. Captain Hanes asked the lieutenants to state which shift they wanted. My first request was to work the evening shift at the Federal Detention Center, but this was given to a new lieutenant despite my seniority. My second request was to work the day shift at the Federal Detention Center, and this request was given to another lieutenant who had less seniority than me. My third request was to work the midnight shift at the Federal Detention Center."

When I asked Captain Hanes why he hadn't honored my shift requests, he told me he wanted me to work around him. "If this is the case," I asked, "why did you assign me to work midnight when you work the day shift? How in the hell can I work around you when we work opposite shifts?" This was some bullshit excuse that made him look like a pure jackass.

CHAPTER 8

EEO Complaint P-2001-048: Discrimination Retaliation Continues

The pressure was still mounting, but I kept fighting and continued to read Psalm 35. My favorite line was, "Fight against those who fight against me."

On October 11, 2000, I wrote another EEO complaint alleging reprisal, retaliation, discrimination, harassment, the use of insulting and obscene language, and misuse and abuse of authority. In this memo, I wrote:

My name is Garry L. Jones, and I am a lieutenant at the Federal Correctional Institution located in Tallahassee, Florida. I have been a lieutenant for seven years. From March 1997 to the present, I have been the victim of racial discrimination, harassment, reprisal, and mean-spirited indifference.

On August 14, 2000, I filed an EEO complaint against Derrick Hanes, chief of correctional services, for retaliation and discrimination. A month later, he summoned me to his office and issued me a performance log with an unsatisfactory entry. It stated that on September 8, Lieutenant Jones ordered the release of two inmates from the Special Housing Unit without authorization from the SRO (Segregation Review Officer).

Captain Hanes spoke with me and stated he didn't want any inmates released from the Special Housing Unit on weekends. He also sent out an email to all lieutenants after issuing me a negative log entry, instructing them not to release any inmates from Lock-Up. This was done to cover his tracks so it wouldn't appear he was singling me out. However, there is nothing in policy that states inmates can't be released from Lock-Up on weekends.

Nevertheless, I honored Captain Hanes's wishes and did not release any more inmates on weekends.

On September 14, while assigned to work the evening shift, Captain Hanes called me to his office. He claimed that he thought he told me not to release any inmates from the Special Housing Unit on weekends. The captain stated he'd been in a meeting with the warden and was caught by surprise when she inquired about two inmates released from Lock-Up six days earlier.

I explained that I couldn't recall releasing any inmates from Lock-Up on weekends. Mind you, the lieutenants keep a log of everything happening on their shift, and the captain has to sign off on it. In this case, he hadn't even bothered to read it.

Whenever he had a meeting with the warden, she would ask him questions. If he couldn't answer one, he always tried to pin the blame on me.

In this instance, Captain Hanes told me I was lying. I explained that I released two inmates on Friday evening. At that time, Officer Chris Wilson was acting as activities lieutenant and could verify this information. The captain claimed he considered Friday evening to be part of the weekend, but I countered that weekends are typically viewed as Saturday and Sunday.

Hanes responded that before I admitted an inmate to the Special Housing Unit, I should complete my detention orders—explaining why an inmate was being transferred—and call him at home.

I pointed out that Wilson completed those orders and that my shift often gets hectic, especially when I'm short-staffed, so I might not have a chance to notify him every time I made a supervisory decision. This is a prison, where incidents can break out at any time, requiring me to make quick decisions.

Hanes insisted that if I didn't have a chance to call him at home, I should send an email to him and the special investigative lieutenant explaining my decisions.

On September 14 at 6:35 p.m., I admitted two inmates to the Special Housing Unit, with acting Activities Lt. Chris Wilson handling the paperwork. For the remainder of the shift, trouble kept jumping into my lap, but I sent both the captain and the special investigative lieutenant those emails. I always keep the captain aware of what's going on at the institution—not because he asked, but because it's how I operate.

According to the institution's policies, the warden delegates authority to place an inmate in administrative detention to the lieutenants. I didn't have to inform anyone of my reasoning for placing an inmate in detention—that's the rule. The lieutenants review available information and determine whether an inmate's detention is justified.

Inmates are placed in detention when their presence among the general population poses a serious threat to other inmates or staff or to the security or orderly operations of the institution. The rules also state that inmates are released from detention when the original reasons for their placement cease to exist. Ordinarily, these reviews are conducted by the captain, but the warden may designate other staff—such as the operations lieutenant of the Administrative Detention Unit or members of the inmate's unit or team—to conduct this review.

The regulations state that operations lieutenants are responsible for making decisions based on their understanding of corrections and past experiences handling the inmate population and unusual incidents. I had more experience than the captain.

The bottom line is that it was my responsibility to maintain the overall security of the institution by monitoring what was happening and enforcing BOP policies and procedures. This included enforcing inmate discipline and behavior, monitoring inmate activities, counseling staff and inmates, investigating incident reports, and preserving evidence while collecting documentation during routine or emergency situations.

As a BOP employee, when I believe my rights have been violated, I'm allowed to seek administrative relief. I got singled out, constantly harassed, retaliated against, threatened with the loss of my job, and assigned various tasks that other supervisors were not required to perform.

I was disrespected by Captain Hanes through his use of obscene and provocative language when he called me a liar—and I know I'm telling the truth. This constitutes a violation of BOP rules.

CHAPTER 9

Singled Out: The Proof is in the Pudding

On Nov. 6, 2000, when Lt. Caldwell reported for the midnight shift, Lt. Carr had admitted two inmates to Lock-Up. Caldwell asked if he'd called the captain to inform him about it. Carr said he had called, but the captain advised him that he didn't need to call him at home when admitting inmates to the Special Housing Unit. Carr also mentioned that the captain told him this only applied to a "certain lieutenant."

I couldn't understand why he would establish different rules for different lieutenants. We were all supposed to work together under the same rules and regulations. If you can recall, Captain Hanes gave me an unacceptable rating on Sept. 22 for not calling him at his house after admitting and releasing inmates to the Special Housing Unit. But on Oct. 19, Lt. Rodriquez did the same thing and didn't bother writing the captain a detailed memo explaining why. Rodriquez didn't receive an unfavorable rating for this. In fact, he didn't face any consequences at all. This only goes to show that Hanes had a different set of rules for different lieutenants.

The captain had me redoing lieutenant modules that I had already completed; I had scored very high on all of them. On Oct. 21, while completing an Inmate Discipline module, I questioned Special Housing Unit Officer Harry about the unit's policies. The reason Captain Hanes had me doing this was that he claimed I didn't understand the Lock-Up procedures. I asked Officer Harry if he was still going downrange with both sets of keys, and if the range door to the unit was still unlocked. This was a direct violation of policy. If two officers go downrange with both sets of keys and the inmates get hold of those keys, they could hold the officers hostage and take over. Policy states that only one officer is allowed to go downrange with one set of keys; if one officer is held hostage, the other officers can lock the range door to prevent the inmates from taking over the whole area.

I informed Officer Harry to discontinue this practice until further notice.

On Nov. 9, while visiting the Special Housing Unit, I noticed Harry downrange with the number two SHU officer, and both range doors were open and unlocked – a violation of the rules since at least three officers were supposed to be working there at all times. I asked Harry why he hadn't followed my instructions, and he responded that the captain told him not to change any procedures in SHU, regardless of what I said.

The Special Housing Unit was not in compliance with policy and procedures, and this only goes to show that Captain Hanes would do anything to undermine my authority.

CHAPTER 10

Riding Dirty

One day, while relaxing in the basement, drinking a cold beer and playing with my dog Sparky, someone upstairs called out, "Dad, Lieutenant Josh is on the phone." It's worth noting that Lieutenant Josh is one of the quietest, humblest, and most spiritual friends I've ever had, second only to Minister Holloman. The only time I've seen Josh upset was when he realized I was being set up. He went to several wardens to explain, "Lieutenant Jones is one of the brightest lieutenants we have, and the vicious lies being spread about him are unjust. You can check his work; this guy knows policy like the back of his hand." I spend time with Lieutenant Jones every day, and some of the accusations against him are utterly ridiculous. For instance, they claim he allowed inmates to run around when the compound was closed—when in fact, he wasn't even at work; he was home recovering from rotator cuff surgery. I know this because I took him for the procedure. For some reason, the captain doesn't like him. The warden's only response is, "I have to support my captains." The fact that they didn't listen to Josh will soon come back to haunt them.

Josh later told me that one of the wardens I worked for admitted, "I regret listening to the captain because she doesn't know anything; she wouldn't know how to get herself out of a paper bag. Josh, I should have listened to you, and now I'm stuck with a Special Investigative Agent who doesn't know a thing, and none of the inmates like him."

"You cannot be an effective agent without establishing a rapport with inmates and staff members," remarked Lieutenant Jones, who ranked #1 among the applicants for the Special Investigative Agent position. Upon reviewing his record, it was noted that he had been recognized as the Correctional Officer of the Year several years ago. He subsequently advanced to the position of Lieutenant, and Warden Flowers appointed him as a Senior Lieutenant at the Federal Correctional Institution in Tallahassee. Prior to his current role, he served as a Special Investigative Supervisor.

Despite being ranked #10, I chose Lee Merrit, a Special Investigative Agent who was perceived as lazy and unintelligent, for the position. During our morning meetings, Lieutenant Josh was tasked with providing updates on all ongoing investigations within the institution. It was clearly stated that Agent Merrit was not welcome in my office due to concerns raised by supervisors in the Regional and Central offices regarding his biased investigations.

Inquiring about Lieutenant Jones, the warden asked, "Didn't he previously work for the D.C. Department of Corrections

(Lorton)? Do you think he would be willing to speak with me?" I was uncertain about Warden Garry's willingness to facilitate the interaction, as he could be quite obstinate, especially when he strongly believed in something. Warden Garry operated based on integrity and principles, and any involvement with the captain was likely due to a personal request for assistance.

She turned away from Lieutenant Jones and began listening to the white lieutenants who would ultimately lead to her downfall.

"Lieutenant Josh, do you think Lieutenant Jones will withdraw the EEO complaint he filed against the captain?"

"I doubt it, Warden. Lieutenant Josh, his EEO complaints are solid. I can vouch for this because I previously worked in the EEO division at the Central Office."

The warden, attempting to engage in casual conversation, mentioned the D.C. Department of Corrections. I recall informing D.C. authorities that they were appointing an incompetent warden. Consequently, the warden's tenure in D.C. was short-lived, lasting less than a year before his departure.

It is said that God has a way of turning your adversaries into stepping stones.

"What's happening, Josh? I'm feeling quite agitated at the moment as I drive back home."

"Is everything alright with your mother?"

"My mother is still unwell, but I have a pressing issue. Garry, I received a call from a superior instructing me to remove my son from Tallahassee as soon as possible."

"I'm not following, Josh."

"Garry, Josh Jr. has landed himself in serious trouble. He

sold marijuana to an undercover agent at our residence."

"Oh no! This is concerning because we reside in staff housing. This constitutes a federal offense, and you could lose your job."

"I am aware, Garry. I have never been this distraught."

"What do you need me to do?"

"Garry, I really need your help because Josh Jr. has drugs in my house."

"Oh no, they are going to raid my house tomorrow."

I can hear Josh Jr. in the background reassuring his father that everything will be okay. "Shut the hell up, Josh Jr.! Where are the drugs in my damn house?"

Josh Jr. replied, "The drugs are under the pillows on the couch, and the gun is under the couch."

"Jr., you have a damn gun in my house! What else is in my house, Josh Jr.?"

"Dad, that's it."

"Josh, how did you not know about this? You are the Special Investigative Supervisor."

"I know, Garry, but the guys in the office bypassed the rules and failed to inform the warden until the FBI contacted him and said, 'The bust is scheduled for tomorrow.'"

"Garry, the warden was completely unaware of what was happening."

"Josh, only the warden can authorize anything."

"Garry, these individuals are worthless; they believe that African Americans in leadership positions are incompetent."

"Josh, are you telling me that your colleagues in the Special Investigators Office, whom you work with daily, didn't inform you about your son's situation?"

"Josh, I warned you about those individuals. I can understand them doing this to me because I confront them when they make mistakes, but Josh, you are the most reserved person at the institution, and you always comply."

"They are aware that you are at risk of losing everything and potentially facing charges yourself. Garry, you know that the lieutenant who is always by my side—the one you dislike and who smirks at me every day—is also involved in this."

"Josh, we don't have time to delve into that now. I have a plan to retrieve the drugs and the gun. Here's what I'll do: I'll head to the basketball court in front of your house around 5:15 p.m. I'll pretend to shoot hoops but intentionally miss the rim, allowing the ball to roll..."

"As it starts to darken around 6:00 p.m., I'll repeat the same act, letting the ball roll into your yard. This time, I'll pick it up, make my way to your back door, and slip inside. By the way, I'll be wearing my favorite black Air Jordan sweatsuit with red accents on the arms. In the darkness, it will be difficult for anyone to identify me since there's no streetlight in your yard. I believe I can navigate inside your house using the light from my cell phone."

"Garry, please be cautious as you are risking not only your job but also your family."

"Josh, I'll contact you once the mission is accomplished."

"10-4, Garry."

Two hours later, I dialed Josh's number again.

When Josh answered the phone, I asked, "Is the mission complete, Garry?"

I replied, "Yes, but I ended up staying in the house longer

than I had planned."

"What do you mean?"

"Josh, I discovered that your son had over a pound of marijuana in the house. When I attempted to flush some of it down the toilet, the toilet got clogged. It took me ten minutes to locate your vacuum cleaner."

"Why did you need the vacuum cleaner, Garry?"

"Josh, while trying to retrieve the drugs hidden under the couch, the bag containing the drugs tore on the couch spring and spilled onto the carpet. I eventually found the vacuum cleaner in your bedroom and cleaned up the carpet."

"I eventually found the vacuum cleaner in your bedroom and cleaned up the carpet."

"As I was heading toward Lake Jackson, I noticed the police presence, so I waited in the car until they left."

"What were you doing at Lake Jackson? People who go there are usually there to make out, Garry."

"I wasn't there to make out; I was throwing out. My intention was to dispose of the drugs and the gun in the lake. Once the police departed, I successfully completed the mission."

"Thank goodness. Garry, I owe you my life."

"No, Josh, I know you would have done the same for me."

"I'm grateful, Garry, especially considering your marital issues. If you had been caught, your family would never have forgiven me."

"I'll give you a call tomorrow after work, Josh."

After finishing work, I called Josh, and he answered, "Is everything alright, Garry?"

"Josh, those individuals who set you up had the audacity

to inquire about your whereabouts. I informed them that you had to unexpectedly leave town because your mother was unwell, and you had taken Josh with you to care for her. I maintained a smile while speaking to them. Upon my return to work the following day, they inquired about your mother's well-being. I assured them that she was doing exceptionally well and that Josh Jr. would be enrolling in school and staying with her to assist. I couldn't help but smile even wider and remarked, 'Today was a good day.'"

"Josh, that's when they realized that I had cleared out everything from the house."

"Why did you tell them it was a good day, Garry?"

"Josh, when they conducted the raid on your house and found nothing, it was indeed a good day because we outsmarted those individuals."

"Once again, I want to express my gratitude, Garry, for saving my life."

"Don't mention it, Josh; I've got it under control. When you come back to the institution, I need you to sign your name on my yearly evaluations because the Captain has a disdain for me, and the officers are not going to be rewarded if my name is on their evaluations. Those officers worked their asses off, and they need to be recognized for their outstanding work."

"No problem, Garry!"

"Josh, have you spoken to the Warden?"

"Yes, Garry; she informed me that she would be transferring me back to the institution here."

"I'll miss having you around, my friend, but I'll make sure to visit you. And when I do, I'll pay a visit to the King."

"Goodness, Garry, which King are you referring to?"

"Josh, I'm talking about Elvis."

We both erupted into laughter.

"Garry, you're aware that they're coming for you?"

"Indeed, Josh, I am aware, but I'll manage.

I'll be attending the Super Bowl in two weeks, and when I come back to the institution, I will buckle down and prepare for the retaliation. I'm used to their dirty tactics."

"Take care, Josh; I'll catch up with you soon."

The sweatsuit I had on when this incident occurred.

CHAPTER 11

Super Bowl XXXIV - Rams vs. Titans

Going to the Super Bowl is like having an addiction: once you go the first time, you'll crave going back. I'll never forget when my brother Pete and I went to our first one, the 35th Super Bowl in Atlanta – the Tennessee Titans versus the St. Louis Rams.

I got a call from my cousin Ann one night; she was staying in Atlanta and asked if I wanted to go to the Super Bowl.

"Damn right I want to go! Do you have tickets?" I asked.

"I know someone who has tickets," my cousin said. "I'll meet you in Atlanta on Sunday morning."

When I got up that morning, I called the captain to ask for sick leave, but I didn't get an answer. When a lieutenant is sick, the proper protocol is to call your captain as soon as possible – preferably eight hours before you're scheduled to work, giving him enough time to find a replacement.

Next, I called the institution to speak with the lieutenant on duty and told him I wouldn't be reporting to work that day because I was sick. When he asked what was wrong, I said it was none of his business because I wasn't obligated to reveal my health problems to anyone. I told him that I had a fever – and I did, the Super Bowl fever – and it would last two days.

He had no clue that I was on my way to the game. "Okay, Jones. Hopefully, you'll feel better, and I will let the captain know that you called in sick," was all he said.

My cousin Ann warned me to be careful when I got close to Atlanta, because they were experiencing an ice storm. I got in my Acura Legend and left Tallahassee. At the same time, my brother Pete was in Charlotte, N.C., driving through local snow, also heading to the game.

We both arrived at Ann's house within minutes of one another. We were supposed to get to the stadium around 3 that afternoon. My brother and I headed out for Campbellton Road Marta Station. When we got there, we hopped a bus and then caught the train to the Dome. The train was packed; I'd never seen so many people in my life. When we reached the Dome, I suddenly heard someone say, "Garry?"

I turned and said, "What's up, Perry?"

"Are you ready to get in the game?" he asked.

"You damn right, Perry," I replied.

Me, my brother, and Perry went somewhere safe to take care of business. Ten minutes later, we were inside the Super Bowl. This wasn't exactly my childhood dream – that had been to play in the Super Bowl. But since I wasn't good enough for the pros, I settled for just being there in the crowd. Celebrities were all around me, having a good time. My mind was now far away from the issues happening to me at work, and life was beautiful for 48 hours.

The game went down to the wire. Tennessee quarterback Steve McNair was two inches shy of getting that ball into the end zone with no seconds left on the clock. Everyone in the game was on their feet. The St. Louis Rams won the game. After Pete and I left, we went outside to buy souvenirs. Prices change dramatically after the game because vendors are trying to get rid of their merchandise.

We didn't have time to stay in town two days post-game to snag Super Bowl souvenirs for 75 percent off. Pete and I grabbed a few things for Ann and some friends, then the next day we both got back on Campbellton Road, with me taking Interstate 75 south to Tallahassee and Pete heading to Charlotte. I was on a natural high now; this high gave me enough energy to go back into the war zone.

CHAPTER 12

The Day My Wife Left Me

When I arrived back in Tallahassee, I was still having problems at work – as well as in my marriage. I was determined to be who God made me: a warrior. My supervisor and my wife couldn't change that. I stood up for what I believed in. Some people want you to bow down to them, but the only person I was bowing down to was God. I lived by integrity and principle.

Most people thought I was going against the grain, and if that's wrong, I didn't want to be right. My wife was determined not to let me be a man; when she couldn't change me, she left with my children Latoya and Malcolm. My oldest son, Derrick, stuck around, either with me or with his girlfriend, Sherrie (R.I.P.). He was attending Florida A&M University when he should have decided to go to North Carolina Central University like his father.

The only one left was my dog, Sparky. He didn't care whether the family left or not; he just wanted me to himself. Sparky was spoiled as hell. He was a white poodle and didn't want anyone next to me. He cried when I left for work and again when I came home at night. He would come into my room and lay beside my mattress.

Me Feeding Sparky

My wife had taken everything, and I was still giving her $550 a month while paying my own rent. I also had to pay Sparky's veterinary bills. Finally, I had some type of peace and didn't have to worry about anyone nagging the hell out of me. But the on-the-job fighting hadn't let up.

My daily routine included running on the track to get my weight down for the Law Enforcement Games. I often took Sparky with me to the weight room and let him sit in his cage and watch me work out. Sometimes having a pet is just like having children; you have to raise them as well.

After my workouts, I would put steaks on the grill for me and Sparky. When I'd reach for the charcoals, Sparky would do a little dance, jumping in the air and snatching at the bag as if he wanted to put the charcoals on the grill himself. I think he knew he was in for some good eating.

On my days off, I'd train twice a day because I had already won a national title in the 198-pound weight class for bench pressing, which qualified me to compete in the International Law Enforcement Games in Barcelona, Spain, in October. I had never been out of the country, so I was getting excited.

When I worked out, I often popped some pain pills to get through it. I knew I needed shoulder surgery to repair my rotator cuff, but I wanted to wait until after the competition. My doctor wouldn't give me any more cortisone shots.

One day, while at the gym, I put 405 pounds on the bench and lifted it once until I felt the inside of my shoulder ripping. My mind was set on ignoring the pain. The next day when I hit the gym, it was too painful for me to lift 225 pounds. I finally accepted that I was not going to Spain. I had paid my money for the competition, but I hadn't booked a flight – and I was glad. With my shoulder being injured, it was hard to concentrate. Weightlifting had taken a lot of stress off me and helped me cope with a failing marriage and work stress.

When I got to work, I always had a smile on my face, even in times of adversity. Those bastards didn't know they were wearing me down. I stood up to them like David stood up to Goliath. I kept reading scripture in the parking lot before I started my shift.

My daughter Latoya was 15 years old at the time, and I knew she was going to bug the hell out of me about getting her a car when she turned 16. One Sunday, I went out car shopping with the intention of pricing one for her. I knew I had a year to look for a car, but I was bored that day. As I browsed the different prices, a thought came to my mind: Let Latoya have my car when she turns 16 and buy myself a new one instead.

I already had my eye on a 525 BMW. I found the car, tested it out, and really liked it. "You looked good in that car," the salesman told me.

"I know, but I'm not going to buy this car until next year when my daughter turns 16," I nodded.

I left the car lot and headed home. My family was still gone, but I knew Sparky was probably upset because I'd been gone for a long time. Before I could get to the next traffic light, I noticed a car following closely behind me. I looked, and it was a brother in a BMW. He kept following me and flashing his lights, but I wouldn't acknowledge him. The brother drove his car around me and started waving to pull over. I didn't know what he wanted, but I thought, If he tries anything, I'm going to tear into his ass.

I pulled over and jumped out of the car quickly. Before he could open his door, I yelled, "What in the hell do you want with me?"

This brother got very nervous and said, "Slow your roll, I'm just trying to sell you a car."

"How in the hell did you know I was looking for a car, and who are you?" I demanded.

"I was on the car lot when I saw you test drive a BMW, and I know a place in Albany, Georgia, that has good prices on cars," he said. "They have a Lexus LS400 for a real good price." I explained that I didn't need a car until next year. He handed me his card – his name was Jonathan – and asked me to call him when I needed one. The brother kept bothering me about this Lexus and asked if I had time to follow him to Albany. I said no since Albany was about an hour and 45 minutes from Tallahassee. I told him to take my number and call me next year, then I left.

The next morning, my cell phone rang - it was Jonathan. I told him I didn't want a car, but he asked me to come take a look at one. "Since you're bothering the hell out of me, I will call you next week on my days off and meet you in Albany, Georgia," I said.

The following week, we met at the car lot and headed off to Albany. He was all smiles when I got there. He had six Lexuses lined up. I got into a grey Lexus and drove the car – it rode well. But I told him I couldn't afford it right now. It was probably a 1999 Lexus.

"Maybe if I can find a Lexus around 1993, I'll consider it," I said.

"What you just drove was a 1993," he responded.

"Stop bullshitting me," I said. He told me the other five were 1995, 1996, 1998, 1999, and 2000. "The one I drove looked the same as the rest of them," I said.

"I know," he nodded.

The Lexus dealership hadn't changed the body of their cars in eight years, he noted, and the 1993 Lexus was a little bigger in the back than the rest of the models. I told him I couldn't afford to buy the car.

"You haven't asked me the price," he said.

I told him I didn't want to know the price – I couldn't afford it. Jonathan told me he could give it to me for around $14,900.

"I still can't afford it," I joked. "I'd take it off your hands for $10,900 out the door, taxes and tags included."

"Man, I can't give you this car for that amount," Jonathan said. "Come on, Garry, work with me."

"I'm not looking to buy a car until next year," I said, and left the lot to head back to Tallahassee.

I called the Tallahassee Credit Union and asked them to price a 1993 Lexus with 199,000 miles on it. They said if the car was in good shape, its blue book value was $14,900 – to my surprise, Jonathan was on the up and up.

The following week, Jonathan called me and said he was able to get the price down to $10,900, but I had to pay for the taxes and tags. I replied, "No, you all have to pay for them."

"Come on and pick the car up, and I'll have someone in the finance department finance you," he urged. Before I left to pick up the car, I called the credit union, and they agreed to finance it as long as the price wasn't above $14,900.

Jonathan didn't know the credit union was financing the car. When I arrived back in Albany and met with the finance department, they asked me what I wanted my payments to be, and I let the salesperson do all the financial paperwork.

I told the salesperson in Albany that I'd decided to let the Tallahassee Federal Credit Union finance my car, and they were willing to cut a check right away. The guy in the dealership's finance department turned red in the face, but he was trying to keep his composure. The reason: he was under the impression that I wouldn't be able to find anyone to finance the car, and his company would do it at a high interest rate. This was the oldest trick in the book.

I drove the car home, picked up Sparky, and we went out riding. Two months later, my wife moved back into the house.

She didn't ask to come back; one day I was at work, and when I returned home to pick up some medication I'd forgotten, the next thing I knew, my family was moving back in. The only reason I accepted my wife and kids moving back was that my kids had gone through enough. I did my best to make their lives as normal as possible.

CHAPTER 13

Super Bowl XXXV - Ravens vs. Giants

It was January 28, 2001, and the Super Bowl was being held in Tampa, where all the hotels were sold out, and the closest available rooms were in Orlando. I arrived in Orlando three days earlier, on January 25—my birthday.

My brother had already made a reservation at the Embassy Suite, but he and the rest of the Super Bowl crew wouldn't be arriving for another day. When I got to the hotel, the valet picked up my luggage and parked my car while I checked into my room, where a bottle of wine was waiting for me—a nice gesture, although I didn't drink wine.

I reached into my bag for my Remy Martin and poured myself a drink. I called my brother in North Carolina to let him know I had checked in.

"Great," he said. "Now pick me up at Orlando International tomorrow morning. How is the room?"

"Lovely," I said.

"Gold," he replied, "don't forget to leave a tip in the morning."

"Pete, I got this. I don't mind leaving a tip," I said. "Hey, Pete, guess what? They have a telephone in the bathroom."

"No shit?" Pete laughed. "Just don't forget to pick me up."

Later that night, I went downstairs to enjoy the ambience in the lobby and drink a couple of beers. One of the hotel employees asked what I was in town for.

"I'm in town for the Super Bowl, man," I said. He asked if I had tickets. "Of course," I smiled.

The next morning, I picked Pete up from the airport and took him back to the hotel. "Man, this hotel is great," Pete said. "You know we have to pick Shellcat up at the airport later tonight."

Shellcat was coming from Washington, D.C. Pete and I hung out in the room and chatted until it was time to get Shellcat. When he walked out of the airport, Shellcat asked, "Go-Go, when'd you get this Lexus?"

"Man, I got it last year," I said.

Before we went back to the hotel, we drove around Orlando for a while. Of course, Pete had to take out his cigar. He never lit it, but he would walk around with it in his mouth, profiling. Pete offered me and Shellcat a cigar, too, but Shellcat said, "Man, I don't want no damn cigar."

"You might as well take it; you already paid for it," Pete insisted. "It's in the budget—cigars, tips, food, and gas." "Go-Go, I see you are still drinking that cognac. When are Antray and Capp coming to town?" Shellcat asked.

"They will be here later tonight," I said. "They arrived in Jacksonville last night and stayed with Capp's sister, Joyce. They should be here shortly."

As for our agenda, we were tourists and decided to do what tourists do—explore the city. When we finally returned to the hotel, Capp and Antray were there, and they were glad to see us. I was, too—I finally had my drinking partners since Pete and Shellcat didn't drink.

As soon as we got settled in, Antray's girlfriend called me and said, "Gold, take care of my baby." I told her Antray was grown and could take care of himself.

Capp got the party started. He went down to the lobby and found someone who knew where the clubs were. We got in the car and followed some dude to a club in Eatonville, Florida—the oldest Black incorporated township in the United States and the home of Zora Neale Hurston. When we got there, I knew I wasn't going in that place. I told them they could go ahead, but I didn't like the environment. Capp, Antray, and surprisingly, my brother Pete—all went in. Shellcat and I went to a nearby Steak & Shake for breakfast.

I told Shellcat, "Man, let's go get the fellows and head back to the hotel." When we returned to the club, the guys were standing outside, wondering where we had gone. We loaded up and went back to the hotel.

The next morning, we planned to attend the Zora Neale Hurston Festival of the Arts and Humanities. While we were eating breakfast, the Miami Heat basketball team walked in from practice and sat down to eat. They were in town to play the Orlando Magic. While we were eating, the Heat's assistant coach, Bob McAdoo, a North Carolina native, looked over and asked me if I had attended A&T University. I told him no, the reason I was wearing the A&T shirt was that I liked to sleep on them.

"Are you all visiting?" he asked.

"Sir, I went to North Carolina Central University, and my brother Pete, who is seated on my left, went to A&T," I said.

"I'm from Greensboro, North Carolina," he said.

"I know who you are, Mr. McAdoo," I said. "You are one of our homeboys. When I was small, I remember you used to shoot the lights out when you played for the University of North Carolina, and you did the same thing when you played for the Lakers."

"My sister taught school in Durham," he said, and McAdoo asked whether we were visiting Orlando. I told him no, we were there for the Super Bowl. After talking with McAdoo, the fellows and I chatted with some of the basketball players. Pete came up with the brilliant idea for me to ask McAdoo for some tickets for the game being played between the Magic and the Heat.

"Pete, you always want me to hustle up tickets while you all sit back and chill," I laughed.

"Gold, your public relations skills are great; people love you," he said.

"Don't try to pump me up, Pete," I said.

As McAdoo was getting ready to leave, I said, "Let me holler at you for a minute." McAdoo came to our table, and I asked if he had any tickets for the game tonight. He asked how many I needed, and I said five.

"You know, it's a TV game, and you all need to be there early," he said. "Go to Will Call and give your names; the tickets will be there waiting for you."

The fellows and I were thrilled. We were there for the Super Bowl, but now we'd also be catching a Magic game. After we got back to our room to shower, of course, I had to get my drink on. After we got dressed, we left the hotel and headed to the Zora Neale Hurston Festival. I got a phone call from another homeboy, Billy Bob (Snitch), who was coming in from Kinston, N.C. He wanted to know where we were because he was about five hours away from Orlando. "Snitch, we're on our way to have some fun," I said. "When you get close to Orlando, give us a call, and we'll come back to the hotel."

The Zora Neale Hurston Festival reminded me of the Black Arts Festival; it was like being at a fair—they had games, rides, and lots of Black artwork. The last one I attended was in Denver when I was training for my job. At that festival, I met Pam, who played on the television show "Martin." I had a pouch with some Crown Royal in it, and she asked for a drink, so I said of course.

"No, I was just joking," she said. "I'm here to sing."

When she got on stage, I can't remember what song she did, but I know it was a gospel number, and she really turned it out. Beetie Bee could sing.

A few hours later, I got another call from Billy Bob, who said he was 45 miles outside of Orlando. I told the fellows we needed to go.

Shellcat said, "We are not going anywhere."

"Shit, I'm driving," I said. "We will get to the hotel when we get there."

Capp said, "Gold, we're going to start leaving you at the hotel because you always want to stay in, and we have to leave and mess up our fun for you."

We went back to the hotel to meet Billy. I told him we needed to get to the arena for the Orlando Magic game. "You all got tickets?" he asked.

"Yes," I said. "Bob McAdoo left our tickets at Will Call."

A few minutes later, we were heading to the game, and when we arrived, not only did Bob McAdoo leave us tickets, but he also left us passes to meet the players and their families afterward. We even had a chance to shoot jumpers on the court after the game.

Sunday morning was the big day—Super Bowl Sunday— and everyone was excited. Tampa was only an hour away from Orlando. We left around 1 p.m., loaded up the car with drinks, and headed to Tampa. When we arrived, the city was jam-packed with people. We parked our car ten minutes from the stadium in the yard of someone charging $25 for parking. The guy was also grilling food to sell to the people who parked there; they even picked oranges from their tree and gave them to us as a souvenir. After we finished eating, I got a phone call from Perry, telling me to be at the stadium by 3 p.m. to pick up our tickets.

You meet a lot of celebrities at the game, and before we went in, we met Magic Johnson. We had fun at the game, and as always, we waited afterward to buy souvenirs because the vendors had to get rid of their merchandise.

The next morning, we got up, ate breakfast, took pictures, and greeted each other. Capp and Antray left for North Carolina. Billy had vacated the place early Monday morning, and I took Pete and Shellcat to the airport. Then I got on Interstate 4 and headed back to Tallahassee.

Is There Anything Illegal About a Brother Driving a Lexus and Going to the Super Bowl?

The Lexus

When I got back to Tallahassee and returned to work, things were still the same. My supervisor hadn't stopped trying to find something I had done that violated policy. He'd been working hard at it, along with the associate warden. They were a team trying to take me down.

Several investigations had been launched against me—from having an inappropriate relationship with a subordinate to not following policy and procedure—but everything had to be dropped because there was no evidence of wrongdoing. This was just a witch hunt because I refused to bow down to them. If they couldn't get me one way, they'd try another. They spread rumors to destroy my reputation; it was hard to do, but when there's a rumor floating around about you, it's amazing how many people believe it.

People love a lie more than they love the truth. The supervisors thought they were slick; they would discuss the investigation around someone in the office, knowing that individual would go out and spread the rumor about me. Some of these rumors even made it back to my home. The supervisors found a way to ensure I had trouble in my own house, and the fact that my wife believed everything negative about me worsened my already failing marriage.

The government knows how to get you one way or another. One day I got a call from my supervisor asking me to come to work to talk with some folks. It was my day off, but I didn't mind coming in. Little did he know, I had a feeling I was coming in to talk with Internal Affairs.

Talking with them can shake the average person up quite a bit, but I knew they were just regular people like me. I put on my Super Bowl hat and T-shirt, got in my Lexus, and drove to the institution. The captain was waiting for me in the lobby.

"Where is Internal Affairs?" I asked.

"How did you know they wanted to talk with you?" he questioned.

"I know this because you always have something up your sleeve," I replied, and his face turned red.

I told the captain that I used to be a special investigator and knew all the tricks. Their tactic was to scare you with that big name, "Internal Affairs"—but I wasn't afraid. Walking into the office, I was met by two agents, one male and one female, who asked me to sit down. They extended their hands to shake, but I didn't respond. A former warden and friend had advised me that when Internal Affairs shows up, they often consult with the warden beforehand to ask how the investigation should go— specifically, whether the warden wanted them to find merit to the charges or to ensure there was no merit to the investigation. They had no clue I knew that. Once they arrived, they had already made a decision about me. Sometimes, when an employee blatantly does something wrong, internal affairs is called, and if they validate the charges, that person might get a slap on the wrist. Not me, though. They showed up to throw the book at me.

When I sat down, they took out their badges as if expecting me to squirm in my seat. Hell, I took out my badge and showed it to them to let them know they were talking to Garry Jones, not some rookie. The badge trick is designed to make your heart race, but if a person is guilty of the charges, their heart will drop into their stomach anyway.

"Mr. Jones, we have to read you your rights," they said.

"Go ahead," I replied. "I'm listening."

The investigation began. I knew if I remained silent, they could use that against me. If you don't say a damn thing, they can conclude you're guilty of all charges.

"Mr. Jones, do you know why we're here?"

"No, I don't know why you are here," I said. "Then again, whatever you all have brought me in for, I won't be surprised."

"Mr. Jones, did you refuse to change your yearly evaluations when the captain asked you to?"

"Yes, I did."

"Why did you refuse to change the evaluations, Mr. Jones?"

"I refused because the captain wanted me to downgrade the officers' evaluations. The evaluations I gave to the officers were fair," I explained. "If the captain wanted those evaluations changed, he could have done so according to policy. He has the right to change the lieutenant's evaluations if he doesn't agree with them because he is my supervisor."

This issue went back and forth for about an hour, with me telling them about policy and them knowing what I was saying was true.

"Mr. Jones, you know you are being investigated for failing to follow policy and procedure and for failing to obey the order of a supervisor," the IA agents said.

"Sir, if this is the case, then what you are investigating me for is not a conduct issue; it is a performance issue that should have been handled at the institutional level," I argued. "When did Internal Affairs start investigating performance issues at the institutional level?"

"Mr. Jones," the agent said, "we ask the questions, and you answer them."

"No, sir, I have a right to ask any questions I want," I responded. "You are bringing charges against me, and you expect me not to ask questions? You must be kidding."

"Mr. Jones, did you allow Inmate Brown to make an unmonitored phone call?" the agent asked.

"I most certainly did," I stated. "I allowed him to make several phone calls in my presence. Where is it in the policy that a senior supervisor cannot allow an inmate to make a phone call? He is my snitch, and his mother passed away, so he was allowed to make a call. But as far as it being unmonitored, I was there when he made the call home, so it was monitored."

"Mr. Jones, this shows favoritism to an inmate and demonstrates having an inappropriate relationship with an inmate," the agent declared.

"I can understand the charge of providing favors to an inmate, but having an inappropriate relationship with a male inmate? How did you get this charge, and where is your evidence?" This was a serious charge that implied some sexual affair was going on between me and the inmate. They never answered my question. They knew they had created some bogus charges against me.

"Sir, as far as allowing inmates to make phone calls—or as you would say, providing favors to an inmate—then you better investigate every staff member here, including the warden, because we all allow inmates to make phone calls," I said.

"Mr. Jones, did you allow an inmate to fax some material from inside the institution?"

"No, I didn't, but if you check the fax machine, it will tell you when a fax is sent out and received," I said. "The fax machine keeps a record of all this. Show me the date and times when I allegedly allowed this to happen and check the roster when I was working to compare it to the time I allegedly allowed an inmate to fax information."

This conversation continued for another hour. They asked the same question in several different ways, and I provided the same answers. Then it got personal.

"Mr. Jones, do you drive a Lexus?"

"I most certainly do, and it drives well," I replied.

"Did an inmate pay for your Lexus?"

"No, an inmate didn't pay for my Lexus," I stated. "Sir, why are you asking me questions to which you already have the answers? I don't have to discuss with you who paid for my Lexus. In fact, you know who is paying for my Lexus because I don't have the title."

"Mr. Jones, I see you are wearing a Super Bowl hat and shirt," the agent said. "Did you go to the Super Bowl?"

"I most certainly did, and I drove the Lexus to the Super Bowl," I replied. "I went last year, and I went this year. I'm planning to go to New Orleans in 2002 for the Super Bowl next year."

"Mr. Jones, how did you get your tickets for the Super Bowl?"

"That's none of your business, sir." These questions were getting outrageous, and IA was overstepping their boundaries. They didn't have anything on me, and I knew it.

"Mr. Jones, you have North Carolina tags on your vehicle when you are supposed to have Florida tags," the agent said.

"Sir, I plan to keep my North Carolina tags. If the police on the street stop me and say it is illegal to have North Carolina tags, then I will have them changed," I replied. "I'm fully aware that when an individual has been in a state for 30 days, they must change their tags. The warden still has her California tags. Did you investigate her?"

"Mr. Jones, is the answer you have given us true?" the agent asked.

"It most certainly is."

"Mr. Jones, are you willing to take a lie detector test?"

"No, I'm not willing to take a lie detector," I said.

"Why not, Mr. Jones?"

"Because I don't have to take one, that's why," I responded.

"But Mr. Jones, this could prove whether or not you are innocent or guilty."

"No, it's your job to prove that, and it's obvious that you don't have anything on me," I stated. "I'm being investigated on four charges when it should be two."

"Why do you say that, Mr. Jones?"

"Because failing to follow the instructions of a supervisor falls under the umbrella of failure to follow policy and procedure," I explained. "And providing favors to an inmate should fall under the umbrella of having an inappropriate relationship with an inmate. As far as I'm concerned, you don't have the evidence to support this serious charge. You haven't asked me a question that should fall under the umbrella of an inappropriate relationship with an inmate—but this is a gray area because providing favors to an inmate is inappropriate, but the relationship part misleads people and shouldn't be included."

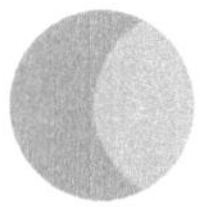

CHAPTER 15

My Response to the Recommendation of 30 Days on the Street

On September 17, 2001, I received a letter recommending that I be suspended from duty for 30 days. I appealed that decision on October 30. My response to the letter was:

"After a careful review of the affidavits regarding the allegations against me, it is obvious that this is a systematic attempt to further harass me. I question whether the same amount of time and work was initiated against all other staff at this facility for the charge of misconduct. There have been numerous incidents of misconduct involving Unit Managers, ISM, and other department heads, including a recent incident of a recreational staff member using not only unprofessional language but also profane and abusive language in the presence of several religious guests standing in the lobby area at the time of the incident. Were these staff subjected to the same level of investigation as I have been? If the agency was thorough in its investigation, then why do we have a lieutenant assigned to the recreation department? This letter proposing actions against me serves only to harass me, humiliate me, and destroy my professional reputation. This is discrimination as it reveals disparities in treatment.

"Where is your proof for the allegations?

"Fact: There have been numerous incidents of staff misconduct at this facility. The names of the staff involved I will not provide at this time because I'm not a snitch. However, given the appropriate investigation, they will be disclosed, along with the nature of each offense.

"Question: Was the same scrutiny applied to other staff with similar or the same charges or allegations?

"Where are the facts? Where are the so-called copies of the faxes that I allegedly allowed an inmate to receive? The fax machine keeps a record of all incoming and outgoing faxes. This is my evidence—only if you check the fax machine.

"Fact: Other lieutenants have given inmates phone calls and they were not accused of having an inappropriate relationship with an inmate or showing favoritism.

"Fact: Inmates are given phone calls by staff other than me.

"Question: How many calls were made by inmates that day? Were they all given the same amount of scrutiny?

"Question: Is the same scrutiny applied to counselors when they allow inmates to make phone calls? Are they charged with inappropriate behavior or accused of showing favoritism? Furthermore, I fail to see any validity in the allegations against me. They are unfounded, unsupported, and without merit.

"As for the charge of failing to follow instructions from a supervisor, one of the responsibilities of a lieutenant is to monitor the performance of the staff assigned to their shift. We are also responsible for initiating and completing performance evaluations based on our perception of their performance. Captain Hanes has repeatedly stated that he does not want to see generic performance entries, yet when I submit my evaluations for his signature, he does not want to support the ratings I arrive at for the officers and always wants me to change them to a lesser grade.

"Question: Why should I take the time to write the entries when Captain Hanes is just going to change them? I see this as undermining my authority as a lieutenant. Changing the rating alters the written entry and would constitute, in my opinion, a generic entry. Again, this is harassment. It appears that Captain Hanes has targeted me since he arrived, and I feel this is because of a comment revealed to me by another lieutenant stating that I—and two other lieutenants—were on his list. I have been a lieutenant for ten years, and to be made to redo a lieutenant's module is insulting, but this too is harassment and abuse of authority.

"You have no proof of any misconduct on my part, and to say that I showed favoritism to any inmate is to imply that all other Tallahassee staff should face the same charges because I have not done anything wrong. I have always maintained the highest degree of professionalism and conducted my duties within the scope and realm of my authority.

"Finally, as stated above, this is nothing more than harassment, retaliation, and reprisal due to the EEO reports I have initiated against this agency, and, in my opinion, retaliation from Internal Affairs agent D. Hunter for reporting what I felt was an inappropriate effort on her part to coerce me into saying something that was untrue.

"Other comments regarding my current vehicle, asking how it was financed, what color it is, and whether I drive a Lexus... I have no other choice than to report this incident as an additional EEO complaint. If you believe in your heart that these allegations are true, why am I only being recommended for 30 days without pay? I should have been recommended for dismissal or termination."

CHAPTER 16

The Warden Issues the Suspension

The letter from the warden read as follows:

"Dear Mr. Jones:

On September 17, 2001, you were issued a notice proposing that you be suspended for a period of thirty (30) calendar days for providing favors to an inmate, having an inappropriate relationship with an inmate, failure to follow policy, and failure to follow the instructions of your supervisor.

In making my decision, I have given full consideration to the proposal, your oral response on October 29, 2001, your written response dated October 30, 2001, and the relevant evidence contained in the disciplinary action file, which has been made available to you.

After careful consideration, I find the charges fully supported by the evidence in the disciplinary action file. Your suspension is warranted and in the interest of the efficiency of the service. However, among other factors, because you have been employed by this agency for over ten years and this is your first disciplinary action, it is my decision that a suspension of fourteen (14) calendar days should have the desired corrective effect. You will be suspended effective November 24, 2001, through December 07, 2001. You are to report for duty at your regularly scheduled hour on December 08, 2001."

I was furious at the warden's decision to suspend me for just 14 days. I wanted her to dismiss me or at least give me 15 days on the street without pay. If she had done this, I could have filed with the Merit System Promotion Board, and I would have received an appointment to challenge my case within a few weeks. But if you get suspended for 14 days or less, then I would have to wait at least six months before I could file an EEO complaint. I knew when I filed it, it would take two years to investigate, even though they were supposed to investigate your complaint within six months.

The only good thing about the suspension was that I had time off for the Thanksgiving holidays. When I woke up on Thanksgiving Day, my wife asked me why I wasn't going to work. I told her I had been suspended for 14 days without pay. I really didn't want to tell her this because I knew she believed everything negative about me and wouldn't accept that it was all about politics.

She told me I should "leave those white people alone" and advised me not to stand up for what I believed in. She actually believed I was sleeping with a male inmate. She forgot that we had a Federal Detention Center that housed men—and this is where the alleged incidents supposedly took place.

In December, I received my paycheck, and it was only for $80. On Christmas Eve, my paycheck was another $80. This didn't break me because I had money saved up, all my bills were paid on time, and the children still got what they wanted for Christmas. The fact that I didn't get paid didn't change my life one bit. I continued my same routine—working out, spending quality time with my children, and being nagged by my wife.

I knew I couldn't continue to live in this hell; it was taking a toll on my body. The guys and I had already made plans to go to New Orleans for the Super Bowl in February 2002, and not getting paid wouldn't stop me from going.

CHAPTER 17

Super Bowl XXXVI Rams vs. Patriots

On January 31, 2002, my plane touched down in New Orleans, the Big Easy. My brother Terry "Pete" Jones and my best friend Anthony "Antray" Dixon were already at the airport. My friend Sheldon "Shellcat" Williams' plane landed a few minutes after mine.

We all gathered in the airport lobby and got reacquainted. We didn't have a hotel booked until a few days later because we hadn't managed to make arrangements in advance like we usually do. Normally, after attending one Super Bowl, we immediately make reservations for the following year, but the hotel industry put a stop to that. They knew they could charge as much as they wanted when a big event was in town, and people would pay without question.

I'd like to say my brother Pete had something to do with the hotels being booked in advance. Where there's a dollar to be made or saved, Pete is the one to consult. Pete had already rented a car, and we headed over to our homeboy Jack' house. He was living in New Orleans at the time in a one-bedroom apartment. Jack is the type of friend who doesn't eat out; he prefers to cook or grill his food. There isn't a woman I know who can out-cook him, except for my mother Vergie, Aunt Mavis, Aunt Jean, and my late grandmother, Tessie Jones.

Jack and I have always been into weightlifting. I was glad to be in New Orleans, especially after what I had gone through a few months earlier. It was good to escape an environment that caused me so much pain.

I asked Jack what he had in the fridge. "I don't have the alcohol you drink, so you can take it or leave it," he said.

Needless to say, Jack had some Icehouse beer in the fridge, and he was right—I didn't drink Icehouse. But Antray and I needed a beer, so we had to find a liquor store. Pete and Shellcat didn't drink, so Pete pulled out the cigars and offered everyone what Shellcat would call a 'stogie.' Like Pete always says, "You might as well take one because you've already paid for it."

Jack was a party animal who loved to have a good time. After we got settled in, Jack asked if we wanted to go out. We declined, deciding we might need to sit back and rest. That Icehouse beer had already made me sleepy. When we got up Friday morning, Jack had to work, so we took our rented car, grabbed a map, and drove around the city.

When Jack got off from work, he announced, "We are going out tonight." We all agreed, and we ended up at a famous club in the city.

When we arrived, we saw a limousine pull up to the club, and Cedric "The Entertainer" got out with about five women and went into the VIP area. I wasn't crazy about going in since I wasn't a club person anymore, but since we were with Jack, we decided to join in. We stayed for about an hour and then moved to another club. Jack knew the whole city; he knew people, and people knew him.

My body started to feel worn out from drinking the Icehouse Jack had in the fridge. I really wanted to go back to the apartment. "Gold, don't start that shit," Jack said. "You don't come into town to rest; you come into town to party. We'll take you home, and the rest of the guys are going back out." When they dropped me back at the apartment, I went straight to sleep. I didn't drink anything the next day except water because it was the night before the Super Bowl, and I didn't want to be tired.

When Jack got off from work, I was full of energy. My mind was focused on the Super Bowl and whether I could get tickets for the game.

The U.S. had just been attacked by terrorists, and I knew it would be tough to get tickets. Normally, I would meet Perry at the stadium, but this year, you couldn't get close to it; in fact, parking was a few miles away. This weighed on my mind all day, but we went to several places in New Orleans, and I was sipping on my Tanqueray Gin and my beer—I had stopped drinking the Icehouse beer at Jack's house. This time, I was determined to stay out all night.

Earlier that evening, I contacted Perry for ticket prices. He gave me an astronomical price and I said, "Man, I can't pay that much for tickets," I said.

"Garry, these tickets are going for a heavy price this year," Perry replied. "Meet me downtown, and I'll see what I can do."

When we met, the price still wasn't right, so the fellows and I stayed downtown and hit the casino. My cousin Ann and Perry's wife were best friends. I called Ann in Atlanta and asked her to talk to Toni, Perry's wife, about giving us a good deal on the tickets.

Ann called me back a few hours later and said, "Perry found someone who is willing to give you the tickets at the price you all want to pay."

"Great, now I can enjoy New Orleans," I said.

I came down here for the Super Bowl, and now it looked like we were going back after all. We had a good time downtown, and I felt more relaxed. Pete and the rest of the guys never got stressed because they weren't going to put themselves out there trying to hustle up tickets. Pete doesn't take chances like I do.

The next morning was Super Bowl Sunday, and Perry called to tell me where to meet him. I, Pete, Shellcat, and Antray jumped in the car to head downtown. We didn't get lost because Shellcat could read a map like Michael Jordan could hit a clutch jump shot. We didn't have GPS in our car—Shellcat was the GPS.

I had to handle the transaction because the guys stayed in the car, saying, "Gold, you are a people person; people love you."

"Man, shut the hell up and stop trying to psyche me out," I said.

I met Perry a few blocks from where we parked, and he motioned for me to go down an alley. As soon as we did, a police cruiser drove by but didn't stop. I started to turn around but thought, The guys are depending on me to get these tickets. I made the transaction, got the four tickets, handed Perry his cut, and walked quickly back to the car. No one was going to get those tickets out of my hands, and if the police had stopped me, they'd be running all around New Orleans because I just paid a pretty hefty price for those tickets.

Super Bowl Tickets – New Orleans

When I got back to the car, Pete asked, "Where are the tickets?"

I told him that I couldn't get them because the man wanted more than he originally charged.

"How much more?" he asked.

I said $100.

"Fellows, do you want to pay $100 more for the tickets?" Pete asked. The guys said that was all they were willing to pay; if the man couldn't accept that, then we were watching the Super Bowl at Jack's house.

I told Pete I couldn't afford another $100, and he said, "I will pay for your share if you get your hands on those tickets." I smiled, reached into my pockets, and said, "I got those damn tickets; now let's ride." You should have seen the look on the guys' faces when I flashed those tickets. Shellcat said, "Gold, you ain't shit for fooling us like that."

We drove back to Jack's house with the volume turned up, listening to "North Carolina" by Petey Pablo. This time, everyone lit up their cigars. We were going back to the Super Bowl! It felt good, considering all the stress I had gone through after getting suspended from my job. Once we got to Jack's house, I put away some liquor and beer. I didn't plan to pay $10 for a 12-ounce beer at the Super Bowl.

When Jack dropped us off in front of the Dome, security was everywhere. We were excited, even as we faced bumper-to-bumper people trying to get in. Everyone was being shaken down, even the boxer Evander Holyfield. The guys and I were right behind him. Of course, we had to take pictures. I could hear the white folks saying, "Look at his ear; it doesn't appear that Mike Tyson bit all of it off." When I looked at his ear, it looked the same to me. He must have had plastic surgery because I couldn't tell where Tyson had bitten it.

Garry Just Arriving at Super Bowl – New Orleans

Garry Meets Holyfield at Super Bowl – New Orleans

Man, it felt great being back at the Super Bowl. We went to our seats and took plenty of pictures. During halftime, I wanted a beer because all the excitement made me thirsty. I went back on my word and paid $10 for a beer, but as I was walking back to my seat, someone bumped into me, causing me to spill some. When I turned around to say something, I realized it was the rapper Mystical. He apologized and offered to pay for another beer—but I chose to take a picture with him instead.

"Where are you all from?" he asked.

"I'm originally from North Carolina," I said.

"That's where my friend Petey Pablo is from," he replied.

Me Inside the Super Bowl in New Orleans

Anthony, Garry, Terry, Sheldon - We Checked Into the
Embassy Suites (Background)
After Attending the Super Bowl

We took pictures, shook hands, and returned to our seats to watch the second half of the game. The New England Patriots defeated the St. Louis Rams by kicking a field goal with no seconds left on the clock. That game was better than the Super Bowl in Atlanta.

After the game, Jack picked us up, and we went out to some more clubs. The next morning, Jack had to work, and it was also the day we could check into our hotel. On Monday night, we headed down to Bourbon Street, where all the excitement was. Shellcat had my video camera filming everything.

When you're on Bourbon Street, anything goes, and you see everything from people making music with trash cans to dancing—and a whole lot of breasts. If you give women beads, they will show you their breasts. It was wild. I didn't see any Black women doing this, but plenty of white women were—and Shellcat filmed everything.

I always wonder why white people can go to places like New Orleans or Daytona Beach for Spring Break and do the wildest things—acting drunk and disorderly—and nothing is said about it. But when Black people used to come to Atlanta for Freaknik or Black Bikers' Week in Myrtle Beach, S.C., during Memorial Day weekend and have fun like this, it's the first thing shown on the evening news.

After we left Bourbon Street, we returned to the hotel. The next day, it was on to the Mardi Gras parade in downtown New Orleans. It was cold and raining, so I told the guys to take me back to the hotel because my back was hurting.

"We're taking you back, but don't call us to pick you up when you want to come back out," Pete said.

I returned to the hotel and read my Bible. My back was hurting for real. What the guys didn't know was that I had prostate problems, and whenever it flared up, I'd get chills and pain in my lower back.

The next morning, Shellcat and I had to go to the airport to fly back home. Antray and Pete stayed an extra day in New Orleans. When my plane touched down in Tallahassee, I felt the anxiety of knowing I had to go back into a war zone at home and work.

When I got home, my wife looked at the videotape to see what was on it. She didn't view it in front of me, but I knew I'd hear about it a couple of days later.

"I see you made sure to film women with their breasts out and film their backside," she complained.

I told her to look at the video again, and she'd see me walking away during the same time the women were showing their stuff—and how could I have filmed that when I was clearly in the video?

"This tells you that someone else must have been filming," I said.

A couple of days later, I heard the captain was leaving Tallahassee, but not due to a promotion. He didn't get demoted, either, but I could tell my EEO complaints were being heard.

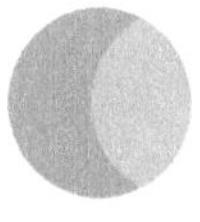

CHAPTER 18

The Captain Leaves Tallahassee

When I heard that the captain was leaving, I was jumping up and down, and I knew my EEO complaint had something to do with him leaving. After all, he was the Bureau's golden boy.

Normally, when a captain has done his time at one institution, he takes the next step up, depending on which direction his career is headed. That step is usually an executive position, but he was going to another institution without a promotion. I know for a fact that this was not what the captain wanted.

In fact, he was returning to an institution where he had already worked. The Bureau was grooming this captain to be the next regional director. If he'd come to Tallahassee intending to truly learn his job—rather than trying to become one of the good ol' boys, meaning he could get away with anything without facing consequences—his career would have taken a positive turn. But he didn't get this way overnight.

He was used to getting everything he wanted without having to pay his dues. When he made mistakes, they covered for him. He worked most of the time as a lieutenant on the day shift with weekends off. He had a very arrogant attitude, and whatever he said went. This would have been acceptable if he'd known policy, but he didn't know shit—and I knew that. Most of the time when he disciplined me, I was acting within policy. You can't come after a man like me when you don't know a damn thing—I will eat you alive.

The worst mistake he made when he came to this institution was to team up with Special Investigative Agent Lee Merritz, who hated me—and I didn't give a damn about him, either. We were both lieutenants at one time, and he was feeble-minded as hell. As a matter of fact, when we both applied for the Special Investigative Agent's job, Lee Merritz was ranked number 10 in scores, and I was ranked number one. Yet Lee Merritz was chosen because one black female captain felt that white was right.

The warden didn't want Lee Merritz in this position either, but he supported the captain's decision. I later found out he said that listening to a captain who didn't know anything was the worst mistake he'd made. The warden was so mad at how incompetent Lee Merritz was that he refused to let the guy give him morning reports. Instead, he requested that the Special Investigative Supervisor provide those reports, which detailed the institution's ongoing investigations of staff and inmates.

The captain, Lee Merritz, and the associate warden were all determined to take me down. When they came after me, there were no rules; they did whatever they wanted, including writing false reports. I remember when it was the captain's last day at the institution. I was working at the Detention Center where the males were located, and I didn't attend his going-away party. I had no intention of wishing him well, but I did want to tell him to go rot in hell.

It was 3:30 p.m., and I was waiting for the lieutenant to relieve me so I could go home. All of a sudden, I had a change of heart about the captain. I told God, "Please take that thought away from me."

That thought was to go say goodbye to him. "No God, I'm not going to do this. This man has put me through pure hell, and you know it." The feeling grew stronger for me to go shake his hand and wish him well. "God, I will do anything except that," I thought, but the spirit within me was so strong that I couldn't do anything but follow what God asked of me. For a minute, I had a change of heart about the captain. I no longer hated him, even though just a few minutes earlier I'd wanted to kill him. I told myself if God wanted me to say goodbye to the captain, then I would.

The captain was in the lobby getting ready to leave. I obeyed God, even though I didn't want to. My mind raced—what are my friends going to say? They knew I hated this man and what he had done to me. When I got to the F.C.I., I was walking inside just as the captain was coming out. I told him I wished him well and apologized for what he and I had gone through. He apologized to me as well, and the last thing he said was that he wished I would drop those EEO complaints against him.

I thought, 'God just told me to apologize to him. He didn't tell me to drop the EEO complaints.' That interaction confirmed my suspicions: my EEO complaints had impacted his promotion.

His mission was to get rid of three lieutenants, and one of them was me. He lied about me to get me suspended, but he couldn't get me fired. To this day, I still wonder why God made me go and make it right with the captain.

CHAPTER 19

The New Captain Reports to the Institution

The new captain was Captain Silverstein, aka "Chester the Molester," another golden boy—but he wasn't as arrogant. He was just a pervert.

I have no idea where he came from—maybe the central office in Washington D.C. The only thing I know is that when he arrived at the institution and saw the female inmates, he immediately got an erection. This man was sick. He never caused me any trouble, but I didn't trust him. Some people who came to Tallahassee were there for two reasons: one was to let you know straight up that they didn't like you, and the other was to try to befriend you. My guard was up, and I didn't trust him.

It was normal for a new captain to show up on every shift to see how it operated, and my advice to any supervisor is to visit all three shifts. This captain was different, though; he'd leave his house and come to the institution all the time between 1 and 3 a.m., even though he had to be at work at 7:30 a.m. The other lieutenants started noticing what he was doing. He grabbed a flashlight and never visited officers in the unit; he would always walk around each dorm with his flashlight, shining it on the women inmates as they slept. Some of the women reported that he'd shine the light in their faces and stare at them while he got a hard-on.

Normally, when people are sleeping, they go to bed in one position and wake up in another, depending on how much tossing and turning they do. Some female inmates sleep with covers on, and some don't. These inmates range in age from 21 to 92. From my understanding, women do have hot flashes; their bodies begin to feel different, so while some opt to sleep without covers, it's due to their temperature.

Notice I said "some." Just because they were in prison didn't mean they lost all self-respect. They were there to do time, not to be used as sex objects. They were someone's mother, aunt, wife, cousin, niece, and grandmother. I often think about the women in my family and how I'd feel if they were incarcerated. I would want them to be respected, especially if they extended respect to the staff.

We encourage female inmates to sleep with covers over themselves because we have male officers who need to do head counts. But when the air conditioning isn't working, it gets hot in the dorms, and those covers come off.

Some female inmates intentionally sleep without clothes on just to excite the officers. They know what they're doing, and it's sad that so many officers have been fired for engaging in sexual activities with inmates.

I must admit that the captain was friendly, to say the least. Later on, I would come to the conclusion that this guy wasn't out to get me; but early on, my guard was still up. I didn't like the way he went after my friend, Lieutenant Walkerfountaine, disciplining her over dumb shit that always came back to bite him. Lieutenant Walkerfountaine and the captain had worked together at another institution as officers. Walker was a smart lieutenant, and she understood policy as well as I did.

As it happened, the captain lived next door to me when I was staying in Federal Housing. I never got a chance to work with the captain much because it was the summer months, and I was working at the Detention Center with the men. When I finally had an opportunity to work with the captain, I noticed he had mismatched black shoes and socks while we were standing on mainline. Where the hell is the Bureau of Prisons finding these captains? Surely, the Bureau couldn't have sent this man after me. If so, I was going to eat this guy alive—he definitely didn't know policy.

I can't make this shit up. How can you respect a man like him? I loved working here because the lieutenants didn't have to do much work. Some people hated working at the Detention Center because it was closed in, but I needed the break.

The lieutenants who worked there didn't have to deal with those female inmates; women don't take no for an answer. They always had "female problems" and would nag the hell out of you. The lieutenants at the Detention Center didn't have to worry about calling for overtime, monitoring the rosters, or finding someone for emergency medical trips. Working at the FDC, you lived longer; but at the FCI with all those women, your chances of dying were greater.

There are differences between working with male and female inmates; for one thing, when you tell a male inmate no, he'll usually go about his business. He doesn't want to be seen talking to an officer. It doesn't look good because some inmates may think you're snitching.

But when you tell a female inmate no, she'll challenge you and she doesn't give a damn if other females know that she's snitching. This was something I wasn't used to; I had spent my career working with male inmates. Adjusting to a female facility was a significant change for me. I thought it would be easier to work with women inmates, but I was wrong, and it was clear the new captain loved it. In July 2002, I had to return to the FCI. I hated it because I knew I wouldn't have any help during the 4 p.m. shift.

CHAPTER 20

Back on the Hill

The lieutenants had to rotate through different shifts and institutions. I had worked at the Detention Center for as long as I could, but now it was time for me to head back to the Federal Institution—or should I say the main institution—where the women were located. Working at the Detention Center for two straight quarters relieved some of the pressure. Even though I had gone through a lot of stress, I was starting to feel good again. I wasn't writing any more EEO complaints, and life had begun to take on a more positive direction. I was beginning to feel like my old self, going to work and doing my job to the best of my abilities, then going home. I wasn't asked to go against policy anymore, and the administration wasn't trying to harass me—at least that's what I thought. But I would soon find out that my days of retaliation were not over.

I may not have been liked by the administration, but I was well respected. They knew they couldn't just do anything they wanted to me and expect to get away with it without a fight. One evening when I came to work, two female inmates were waiting outside my door: a tall white inmate and a short black inmate who appeared to be ten years older than me. She would later tell me that I reminded her of her son. She showed me a picture of him, and we shared some similarities. I asked them what they wanted, and one of them said, "Mr. Jones, we are your orderlies and we are assigned to clean the office."

"Why couldn't you clean the office during the day shift?" I asked.

"The captain has us in his office most of the time during the day shift, and sometimes when we try to clean the lieutenant's office, they treat us mean and say, 'Wait until the 4 p.m. shift, then come in and clean the office,'" the inmate replied.

I knew they were telling the truth because the day shift gets real busy, and it's difficult to leave the office then since most of the administration and staff hang around the lieutenant's office gossiping. They didn't want the inmates to hear what they were saying, so they would advise them to come back and clean during the evening.

I told the inmates that I knew how to clean up my own office, but I let them do the work anyway because my shift was getting busy and I couldn't leave the office. Besides, I never allowed the overnight shift lieutenant to relieve me with a dirty office. There were times when I arrived to find it filthy, with coffee spilled on the floor, trash cans overflowing, and on top of that, the lieutenants who chewed tobacco spat in the trash cans. This was downright despicable.

The captain had put out a memo stating that we had a program review or an American Correctional Association inspection coming up in three months. Whenever we have one of those inspections, the administration work the inmates like slaves. After the inspection is over, the institution returns to normal. They make sure to have the inmates washing, waxing, and buffing the floors, shining the windows, or cleaning the edges of the floors with toothbrushes. They ensure the area where the captain and lieutenants work is sparkling clean during these inspection times.

It was hard for the inmates to accomplish all this during the day shift; too many activities were going on. Sometimes we'd see inmates coming out of the units heading to the lieutenant's office on the overnight shift because they needed to wax and paint. What they couldn't finish on the evening shift had to be completed on the midnight shift. The inmates could wax and buff the floors without staff walking on them and messing things up, but they still had to be supervised.

When I needed to leave the office, I had to lock the door and tell the inmates to come back later to finish the work. I would occasionally manage to escape the office to make rounds, and sometimes when I got a chance, I'd check in with the officers or go stand in the mainline because I didn't have an activities lieutenant working for me; therefore, I was the only lieutenant handling the job of two.

My orderlies would often get disappointed when I told them I'd be back in five minutes so they could finish their jobs—and those five minutes would stretch into three hours. My friend, Lieutenant Walkerfountaine, who worked the day shift, would often visit my office and chat for hours. She would supervise the inmates if I had to attend to an emergency. Lieutenant Walkerfountaine wasn't from Tallahassee, and most of the time she would bring Lieutenant Caldwell and me some chow to eat or take care of unfinished work. My friend, Lieutenant John Coleman, used to stop by my office every time he got off work, but he was eventually transferred back to the Federal Correctional Institution in Memphis. Another buddy of mine, Lieutenant Caldwell, didn't stay in town, so he rarely dropped in to talk, but he would call me from home. I used to tell Caldwell, "Man, I can't talk on this phone; I've got too much going on. You know I don't have any help."

Lieutenant Walkerfountaine was a no-nonsense type; the inmates straightened up when she was around. Usually, when she and I were in the office, we'd discuss personal matters, and the inmates would have to step outside until we finished. Once we wrapped up our personal chat, we'd signal for the inmates to return. I would often bring in my CDs and play Maze and Frankie Beverly while I worked. Sometimes, Walkerfountaine and I would sit back, tell jokes, and the orderlies would start laughing. I guess they needed a laugh every now and then, and they were glad someone was treating them like human beings. I always treated people the way I wanted to be treated.

The medical office was parallel to the lieutenant's office. Certain medical staff would come over to chat with me and Walkerfountaine, and they'd join in on the jokes as well. Sometimes, one of the medical staff would say, "Jones, could we use your orderlies to clean our office?"

"No," I'd reply. "Because you have your own orderlies," but they'd insist their own orderlies were pretty sorry workers.

"The orderlies who work for you keep your office spit and clean," I'd say.

Some staff would get jealous when you had a good rapport with inmates and staff members. I was a people person; it was easy to talk to me. I never let my rank go to my head. Every now and then, I'd let an inmate get away with saying, "Lieutenant Jones, it looks like you may have gained some weight."

I'd respond, "Now that I'm working with you all, maybe I can lose some weight because you all will worry the shit out of a staff member."

When I was over at the Detention Center, the inmates were locked down, and they couldn't come to the lieutenant's office at will unless I called for them. I understood the inmates were speaking the truth about my weight because other officers would tell me I was putting on weight again. After one inmate mentioned my weight, I told her to go to the medical office and inform them that Lieutenant Jones requested the weight scale be sent to the lieutenant's office. When the inmate returned with the scale, I weighed myself, and then Walkerfountaine weighed herself. We both agreed we needed to lose some weight.

The inmates asked if they could weigh themselves. "For what?" I asked. "Both of you look like you're suffering from anorexia." This made them laugh, but I was serious.

This became a weekly ritual. I would send the inmates over to medical to get the scale. Walkerfountaine and I competed to see who could lose the most weight. My orderlies were in competition with one another to do the same.

By 7:30 p.m., Walkerfountaine would say, "G, do you need me to do anything else because I'm going home?"

"Just step outside where other inmates can see you, because when they see you, they're afraid to come to the office and worry the hell out of me," I responded.

The lieutenant's office was set up so the inmates outside could see inside, but if you were sitting down, they could see only your head. When you stood up, they could see who was working.

We also had an office in the back, where Walkerfountaine spent most of her time when she visited me. A person had to come to the lieutenant's office to see the back office. When the inmates came to my office and looked left to see Walkerfountaine inside, they'd say something like, "It's not important, Lieutenant Jones, I'll come back later."

The sad thing about returning to the FCI was the staff shortage and the fact that the inmates were well aware of our problem. They would literally do whatever they wanted, and no one could catch all the illegal activities happening.

The administration wasn't hiring, and while it used to be that one officer would supervise a dorm, they arranged for one officer to monitor two dorms to save money. Some things the administration could get away with in the outside world, but a prison is not a place where they should have staff shortages. When the staff left to check on another dorm, inmates there would be fighting and having sex with one another at will, and there was nothing we could do about it. It was shameful that my friends, who had already completed their shifts, would come over to help me because they knew the administration left me with a short shift, hoping to see me fail.

CHAPTER 21

Another Investigation

I knew it was only a matter of time before another investigation was launched against me for more false allegations. I hadn't been at FCI for more than six weeks before more bullshit went down.

One day when I arrived at work, a black orderly was waiting for me. She asked if she could confide in me, and I said, "It depends on what you're talking about."

"Do you know inmate Bedford?" she asked. "Loud, big-mouth Bedford?" I said.

"Yes," she said. "Well, you need to watch out for her because she is trouble, and I don't want to see another black staff member lose their job."

"What does that have to do with me?"

"Mr. Jones, she will lie to get what she wants."

I actually enjoyed talking with big-mouth Bedford from time to time. Inmate Bedford was well-known on the compound.

Whenever she came to my office, she always had some game—but I was used to that with inmates. One day, inmate Bedford dropped by and said she wanted to talk. I told her to have a seat.

"I need to let you know about one of your officers," she said. I asked what she meant.

"He is dirty," she said.

"In what way is he dirty, inmate Bedford, and why are you telling me this? If he is dirty, you should report this to the Special Investigative Agent (SIA)," I said.

I didn't like SIA Agent Lee Merritz, and I wanted to tell her I wasn't fond of that jackass myself, but I kept it professional. Inmates never wanted to tell Lee Merritz anything; they hated him and didn't trust him. Besides, my Special Investigative days were over. I figured, Let Lee Merritz do his job; that is what his lazy ass gets paid for—but of course, I didn't tell the inmate that.

"Inmate Bedford, what information do you want to tell me?" I asked.

"I have semen from one of your officers," she said. I was stunned. "You have—what!?" I shouted.

"I have some semen from one of your officers," she repeated. "How in the hell did you get some semen from my officer?"

"I've been sexing him for a while," she said. "Your captain has been looking at me like he wanted to have sex with me. He gets his feel on everything now and then."

"No, the hell with the captain," I said. "Get back to talking about this semen you have from this officer—and why are you telling me this? What do you want from me?"

"I don't want anything from you," she said. "I just trust you because you are cool with everyone."

"No, you want something," I said. "What do you want?"

"I don't want anything, Lieutenant Jones," she said. "After your officer got what he wanted from me, he and his other friends have been talking shit, and now he is sexing other inmates."

"How did you get his semen, Bedford?"

"I had oral sex with him, and after he finished in my mouth, I saved it to get that no-good bastard."

"If what you're telling me is true, then where is the semen?"

"It's in my locker at work," she said.

"What's the real reason, Bedford, that you're divulging this information?"

"Because he is sexing another inmate, and he's not bringing my jewelry and Victoria's Secret products anymore," she said.

"Bedford, you need to report this information to the SIA because I'm not going to do his work."

A couple of days later, I approached the officers and told them what was being said. If it was true, they needed to stop this bullshit.

"And by the way, Officer Mike, she said she had your semen," I noted.

Officer Mike's mouth dropped.

"Officer Jason, you need to stop calling that inmate a bitch if what she's saying is true," I said. "And as for you, Eric, she stated that inmate Warsaw has been calling your house and knows your personal phone number. You know the Special Investigative Agent Lee Merritz's job is to investigate blacks, and when whites get caught up in illegal activities, they usually have a chance to resign. But when blacks get caught up in illegal activities, they usually get fired, charges are brought against them, and sometimes they go to jail or get probation."

I had already written Lee Merritz a memo about his biased investigations. I remember clearly when I put Lee Merritz on notice by sending him that memo, which I also decided to send a copy to the warden, associate warden, and the captain. The memo stated, "It has been brought to my attention that you tried to coerce inmates Warsaw and Bedford into making false statements about me by asking them, 'Why are you trying to protect Lieutenant Jones?' I don't care how you conduct your investigation, but don't try to use me to get what you need. If you were more trustworthy, maybe inmates and staff would confide in you. You should put just as much energy into investigating dirty white staff and inmates as you do dirty black staff and inmates. If you continue this practice, you will be dealt with by someone in a higher authority than me."

"Guys, inmates lie all the time," I told the two officers. "As a lieutenant, it's my job to keep you on the right track. I don't want to see you all lose your jobs."

"You are right, Jones; inmates lie all the time," Jason said. Later, Officers Jason, Eric, and Mike would all get fired. A few days later, the associate warden told me to report to her office, and I did.

"I have the memo you sent to the warden about Special Investigative Agent Lee Merritz regarding how he conducts his investigations," she said. "You also threatened him and called him a racist."

"Stop, wait one damn minute," I said. "Show me on that memo where I threatened him."

"Mr. Jones, you said that he should put his energy into investigating dirty white staff and dirty white inmates like he investigates dirty black staff and dirty black inmates," she said. "Yes, I said that, and that was not a racist statement," I responded.

"Mr. Jones, you told him that if he keeps it up, he will have to deal with someone higher than you."

"Yes, I said that, but that was not a threat; that was the truth," I said. "He can't keep going on with this practice before someone with a higher rank than me is going to notice what he is doing."

"Mr. Jones, is this matter dropped?" she asked.

"As far as I'm concerned, it's over," I replied. The associate warden said the matter was dropped and would not go any further.

When I left the A.W. office and returned to my post, my orderly came to the office and said, "Lieutenant Jones, I saw Bedford talking to you again. She is trouble."

"Forget about Bedford," I said. "And by the way, where is my other orderly? She should be here by now. I tell you what: you can go ahead and get started cleaning until the other orderly arrives."

The day shift lieutenant left me with a lot of paperwork, and on top of that, I only had one compound officer. How in the hell did they expect me to run a shift? I was definitely getting tired of this shit.

"Mr. Jones, did you get a memo from the captain?" the orderly asked.

"What memo?" I replied.

"He wanted us orderlies to wax the hallway and the lieutenant's office," she said.

"I don't have the staff to supervise you all," I replied.

My other orderly walked in at that moment and said, "Hi, Lieutenant Jones. We have a long evening ahead of us because the captain wanted us to wash and wax the hallway and the lieutenant's office."

"I know, I heard," I said. "You all can start mopping the hallway."

I called the Control Center officer and told him the inmates would be in the hallway mopping and waxing, and he should keep an eye on them while I go check on mainline (mainline is when inmates are eating). The Control Center officer said, "O'K boss."

"Man, what'd I tell you about calling me boss?" I said. "Don't call me that."

He asked why, and I replied, "Because when the letter BOSS is turned around backward, it stands for 'Sorry Son of a Bitch,' and if that's what you're thinking, you better get that thought out of your mind."

"No, boss—I mean, no, Lieutenant Jones, I'm not thinking that way," he said. "I will make sure I keep a visual on these inmates while you go run mainline. Jones, you forgot about the cameras we have in here. I can monitor them on the cameras." Yes, I had forgotten that. I didn't return to my office until about 7:45 that night, and the hallway floor outside the lieutenant's office was almost dry. One of the orderlies said, "Lieutenant Jones, my colleague and I have worked out a deal."

"What is that?"

"I'm going to mop the lieutenant's office and then go back to watch TV, if that's alright with you, and she is going to wax the office," she said.

This was one day I truly wished Lieutenant Walkerfountaine was here. I really needed her help.

It was now 9:30 p.m., and the compound was closing, getting prepared for the 10 p.m. count. I called the Control Center officer to inform him that I would have one inmate on my count instead of two for the lieutenant's office. The day was really flying by, and I hadn't even completed all of my paperwork yet. By 10:40 p.m., I asked the compound officer how many more dorms she had to count. She said four, and I exclaimed, "Shit, the count is not going to clear until about 11:10." The orderly was in the process of waxing half of the office, so I informed her that the midnight lieutenant would call her out after midnight to finish the office.

I called the medical staff and asked if he had any inmates in his office. He said no.

"Do me a favor: go help the officer count the rest of the dorms," I said.

"No, I can't do that," the medical worker replied.

"Oh yes, you can; I'm giving you an order to go help count," I insisted. "You must have forgotten that after 4 p.m., I'm the warden, and you will do what I tell you to."

Normally I don't talk that way to other staff members, but some white people find it difficult to take orders from a black person. The medical staff went onto the compound to help count. I didn't have a staff person to monitor things while the other staff counted, so I just looked out the window and kept an eye on the compound myself. My mind was made up—since they weren't giving me enough staff to work with, some shortcuts would have to be taken.

Before my orderly left the office, she said, "I really have to tell you something, Lieutenant Jones."

When I asked what the problem was, she said when she works for the captain during the day, he's always having her put plaques on the wall. I asked, "Did he provide something for you to stand on?"

"Mr. Jones, I asked him that, and he said he didn't have anything for me to stand on. When I reached real high to put the plaques on the wall, the captain would come up behind me and grab my waist and help me with the plaques," she said.

When he does that, she explained, she gets sick to her stomach because she can't stand it—but if she tells someone, they won't believe her because she's an inmate. She said the captain always made inappropriate remarks while she did her work, but she wouldn't engage in the conversation.

"He will say things like, 'You must be on your cycle because you are always quiet,'" she said.

"Does he make these statements to the white orderly?" I asked.

"I don't know, because he never made any statements around me when she was present," she said. "But I do know that when he comes out here late at night after midnight, he will come to my dorm to wake me up with a flashlight."

"I'll tell you what; if I'm not busy, you can tell me the rest of this story when I come back to work," I said.

When I reported to work the next day, I noticed the orderlies didn't report to my office. I called the units and told the officers to inform the orderlies to come to the lieutenant's office. Both officers reported that the orderlies were in the special housing unit (lockup) pending further investigation. Rumors on the compound were that I was having an inappropriate relationship with my orderlies. That's why they call them rumors, because I knew that shit wasn't true.

The SIA led people to believe that the inmates were locked up because of me. In a way, that was true, because I eventually learned why the inmates were locked up. I went over to the Special Housing Unit to talk with my orderlies and asked them what was going on. They said they didn't know. The captain had called them into his office earlier that day and informed them that they were being reassigned to other duties. One would work on the compound and the other would handle the visiting room. The captain informed the inmates to get their regular assignments back, but they were not to say anything to anyone else and should not disclose this conversation. The inmates said they reported to their new assignments, and a few hours later, they were locked up pending an investigation.

One of the nosy staff members who had started the rumor about me having an inappropriate relationship with the orderlies later found out that shit wasn't true.

One of my friends who knew some people went to the front office to find out if any of this was true about me, and he was told the investigation had something to do with Jones, but he was not being accused of anything. As it turned out, my supervisor, the captain, was the one being investigated.

I later found out what had happened. That medical worker I ordered to help with the count got mad and wrote the warden a memo stating that I usually got the weight scales for the inmates to weigh themselves, and I'm always in the office joking with the inmates, which was inappropriate. The warden told the captain to change the orderlies' assignments, but he didn't want to; he wanted the warden to change my assignment. The warden said no; the inmates would get new assignments before Jones goes anywhere.

After the inmates' assignments were altered, the captain went to see the warden's secretary and told her to change the two orderlies back to the captain's/lieutenant's office. The secretary said she couldn't change the inmates back to their original assignments without orders from the warden. The captain went to the warden and told her he wanted those two inmates to work for him. The warden said no, but the captain ignored that order and returned to the warden's secretary, demanding she change those assignments.

The warden grew suspicious and decided to call Internal Affairs to have them investigate the captain and the two orderlies. She ordered the inmates locked up pending investigation.

The captain would tell everyone that Lieutenant Jones must have done something for those inmates to get locked up. I couldn't believe some of those feeble-minded staff members believed that. The SIA Lee Merritz was working hand in hand with the captain to shift the investigation off him and onto me. They spoke with the orderlies, who told them I was always professional with them. Lee Merritz asked the black orderly, "Has Jones ever said anything inappropriate to you? And if you tell me yes, I will have you protected. Just tell me—give me something to go on."

She said, "No, but the captain always says something inappropriate to me."

Lee Merritz wouldn't report that information.

CHAPTER 22

Internal Affairs Arrives

I came to the office one evening, and while I was doing the rosters, I discovered I had been changed to Special Assignment, effective the next day. I was given the day watch shift.

I called the captain to ask why I was working the day shift and when he had planned to inform me about this change. The captain claimed he didn't know anything about it.

"You're the only one who can authorize the change, so why are you lying?" I demanded. I added, "I called Lieutenant Stoney and asked him, 'Why the hell did you change me on the roster?' and he said, 'The captain told me to change you.'" I knew Stoney was telling the truth because this captain was a liar. Sometimes I don't even think he knows when he's lying. I put two and two together and concluded that Internal Affairs would be in the institution the next morning. The institution was always trying to be slick by not telling you when the agents were coming in to investigate. I'd been through enough investigations to know the game. They always came in to catch you off guard, but they failed to realize that when you tell the truth, you don't give a damn if they show up or not; the truth will prevail. I didn't have to prepare for that.

I came to work the next morning, sat in my office, and did what I wanted to do. I asked the captain if he had anything for me to do. He said no.

"I guess you still don't know why I'm here," I said, and again he said no.

"You're a liar," I replied. The captain looked at me and turned red—not because of my words, but because he was nervous as hell. He had to find a way to get to those inmates to change their stories and claim I did something inappropriate, but the agents were already in the institution.

The fact that I wasn't supposed to know they were there worked to my advantage. I played it off and went over to the Special Housing Unit where my orderlies were. The captain couldn't tell me I wasn't allowed to go over there because it would blow the agents' cover. When the orderlies saw me, one of them said, "Lieutenant Jones, guess who came over to visit us—Internal Affairs. They are really trying to make us lie about you and say you treated us inappropriately, but we told the truth."

I said, "Ladies, you can't discuss with anyone what those agents talked about. It is against policy. You signed a waiver not to discuss it, or you're going to get yourself in deeper trouble."

"Lieutenant Jones, after they leave, do you think they will let us out of the Special Housing Unit?" one of them asked.

I said I didn't know.

"Lieutenant Jones, that snake of a captain came over this morning before the agents arrived and told us to keep our mouths closed," one inmate told me.

The captain was clearly in violation of policy, and he was feeling the heat—and it was funny to me. When I left Special Housing around noon, I went back to the lieutenant's office and told the captain, "You better tell those agents that if they want to talk with me, they will have to do it after lunch."

The captain still wouldn't admit that any agents were in the institution. He was sweating bullets and said, "Jones, where are you going to eat?"

I told him I was heading to Hungry Howie's Pizza for a steak and cheese sub. He asked if I wanted him to pay for it, and I said no, I had my own money. His nervousness deepened because he knew I understood what was going on—I knew he and the SIA were trying to set me up. He got up and went outside to smoke a cigarette but couldn't even hold it in his mouth.

When I got back from lunch, the captain said, "The Internal Affairs agents are here."

"When do they want to talk to me?" I asked.

"I don't know," he replied.

"You're still lying," I said.

The agents played it cool, first talking with Lieutenant Walkerfountaine about a different issue unrelated to the orderly case. Later, when I met up with Lieutenant Caldwell, he said, "Jones, did you know the Internal Affairs agents were here?"

I said yes.

"They want to talk to me, and it's definitely not about the orderlies issue," he said.

Caldwell, Walkerfountaine, and I were used to being investigated. When the agents first arrived, they might bring up some old issue that happened years ago. This is how I know the SIA keeps an open file on you. Until that file is closed, you're not eligible for promotion, whether you're innocent or guilty. This is how the institution destroys your career, by keeping your file open just for the hell of it. When they can't find anything on you, that open file hurts your career. Of course, you don't know your file is kept open, but they forgot I used to be a Special Investigative supervisor myself.

At 2 p.m., the captain came into my office and said, "Jones, there are some people out front who want to talk with you. If you need me for anything just let me know." What the captain was saying was that if they asked about him, I should lie and say I didn't know anything. This is why the captain was being nice to me.

When I went to the office, the same agents from all my previous investigations were there. They reached out for me to shake hands, but I said, "No thanks, let's get down to business. What do you want with me?"

They read me my rights and then asked me three questions.

"Do you know Inmate Brown and Inmate Marlene?"

"Yeah, I do."

"Have you ever said anything inappropriate to them?"

I said no.

"Mr. Jones, did you threaten the Special Investigative agent by writing a memo stating that if he continues his practice, he will have to deal with someone higher than you?"

"I most certainly did, and that was not a threat," I said. The agent responded that in his opinion, it was a threat. I replied, "Of course, everyone has their opinion."

"Mr. Jones, we looked at all the people who lost their jobs for doing something illegal, and it was an even split in how whites and blacks were treated. Whites and blacks received the same punishment," the agent claimed.

"I don't believe that, and I was told by the A.W. that this matter was closed," I shot back. "But I see that you allowed SIA Lee Merritz to send this investigation in to you all. This is illegal because he's not permitted to send you investigations that apply to him. The warden and the A.W. didn't know anything about it, so he managed to get things past them without their signatures. What the institution needs to do is start bringing in a warden and associate warden who know their jobs."

It took 30 seconds for them to ask me those three questions because the investigation wasn't about me. They then proceeded to ask about a memo I had sent to my lawyer, the office of the Florida Attorney General, and the office of Florida's U.S. Senator, Bob Graham.

The agent said, "We have a memo that you sent."

"What does that mean?" I asked.

The agent replied, "You sent that memo on government time and equipment."

"It was government business," I asserted. "I wrote that memo two years ago, and I know you all have a copy of it."

The agent confirmed they did, and I said, "I have a copy of my own memo. You conducted a biased investigation on me, so I reported it to the appropriate people—that is government business."

The agent responded, "If you have any issues with how we conduct our investigation, it should be kept on the inside; it shouldn't go to the senator."

I told them I could send whatever I choose to anyone I wanted. Then I asked, "Do you have any more questions for me?" They said no. They knew when I left, I would probably send another memo to the senator. The next day, my orderlies were released from the Special Housing Unit. The agents hadn't managed to convince them to lie about me, but they disregarded the information they had on the captain. He clearly had someone high up watching out for him—and it wasn't God. It was someone in Washington, D.C. protecting him because he was getting away with serious shit that the warden couldn't do anything about.

CHAPTER 23

Inmate Brown Tells It All

Inmate Brown approached me in February 2003 and said the captain was still winking at her when she walked by him on the compound, and she wanted something done about it.

"If I report what you told me, this is what's going to happen to you," I said. "The administrative staff is going to snatch you off the compound and put you in the Special Housing Unit pending further investigation. You're going to receive 'diesel therapy.' They'll send you to county jail, and when you're assigned to another institution, it will take forever to get there because you'll be stuck in various county jails.

"Once you get to your destination," I added, "you'll be so far from here it will strain your family to visit. This is what the institution does when you report wrongdoing, and their excuse will be that they had to separate you from the staff member you accused of making inappropriate remarks. Inmate Brown, think about this for a couple of days before you make your decision."

I advised her to come back in a few days, but she insisted on moving forward with her statement, fully aware of what the institution would do to her. While Inmate Brown was in my office, Executive Assistant Carson came by and ordered her to leave, stating that her presence in my office didn't look good. "It gives the wrong appearance," he said.

Carson never liked me, so why was he trying to act like he was looking out for my best interest? I figured he must have been afraid that Inmate Brown would report him for approaching her and calling her a good-looking woman. Brown decided against having me write about that because she had seen too many black staff get in trouble; but Carson was on the borderline of making an inappropriate remark.

The following is what Inmate Brown reported to me, along with the memo I wrote to the executive assistant:

"On Feb. 11, 2003, at 6:15 p.m., you approached me in the lieutenant's office and stated this was the second time you'd seen Inmate Brown in there. I explained that I asked her to come to talk. You wanted to know what we discussed. I explained that she had shared things with me that she was afraid to share with anyone else. I told you that Inmate Brown said she didn't like coming to the lieutenant's office because of how people looked at her. She made this statement because she was under investigation for being too friendly with staff.

I told Inmate Brown that if she hadn't done anything wrong, she shouldn't worry about what staff said. I also explained to you that I wasn't going to change my behavior or communication with inmates because of what people think of me. Staff has never approached me positively—it's always negative. Inmate Brown has never come to my office unless called.

I explained that Inmate Brown shared how Captain Silverstein treated her unprofessionally. She was afraid to report this because when inmates do, they often get sent to the Special Housing Unit or transferred away from their family. Inmate Brown shared the following:

- Inmate Brown stated that on Dec. 18, 2002, Lee Merritz said he would offer her protection from Lieutenant Jones if she would tell him if I said anything inappropriate to her.

- Inmate Brown stated she was in the Special Housing Unit for 60 days and no SIS staff talked to her – but they pulled Inmate Marlene out of her cell every week to talk to her.

- Inmate Brown said she wanted to tell Lee Merritz that Lieutenant Jones didn't say anything inappropriate, but his boss, Captain Silverstein, has done things and said things to her that were inappropriate. She said the reason why she didn't tell Lee about the captain was because she didn't want to be transferred or sent back to Special Housing Unit.

- Inmate Brown stated Captain Silverstein asked her several times what type of men she liked.

- Inmate Brown stated Captain Silverstein asked her three or four times if she was experiencing her menstrual cycle.

- Inmate Brown stated Captain Silverstein told her she was a very nice looking black lady.

- Inmate Brown stated Captain Silverstein told her to wear her shirt inside her pants for him.

- Inmate Brown stated Captain Silverstein ask her if she would wear shorts to work for him.
- Inmate Brown stated Captain Silverstein said she had some nice hairy legs.
- Inmate Brown stated Captain Silverstein would have her and her co-worker put pictures on the wall, and he would stand behind her where he could touch her buttocks. Inmate Brown stated she didn't say anything because no one would have believed her.
- Inmate Brown said the captain told them they were being locked up because of a memo Sumpter had written. Inmate Brown stated Captain Silverstein told them if she told anyone, he would deny he'd said it.
- Inmate Brown stated that when she was living in C-Unit, Captain Silverstein told her that he was coming there at 1 a.m. or 2 a.m. to catch people smoking. Inmate Brown also stated Captain Silverstein said he knew which cubicle she slept in, and he was going to see her and he may touch her on her forehead.
- Inmate Brown stated when she was in Special Housing Unit, A.W. Zane told her she could get out of there if she would tell what she knew about Lieutenant Jones.
  - Inmate Brown stated Captain Silverstein came to Special Housing Unit and told her she could get anything she wanted on the commissary list.

"Mr. Carson, we also discussed Captain Silverstein coming into the institution late at night, walking through the units with a flashlight. This is a regular pattern for him on weekends. We also discussed that when administrative staff hears about workers being unprofessional, nothing is done or it gets overlooked.

We talked about the OIA investigating me for allegedly threatening Lee Merritz by calling him a racist, but no one investigated the captain when he allowed an inmate to call him a cracker. A.W. Zane and I discussed the memo about Lee Merritz and Captain Silverstein, and she claimed it was over. All of a sudden, this new information was sent to the OIA. Where is the trust from your executive staff? They tell you one thing and do another.

It should be noted that Lee Merritz has created a pattern of coercing and intimidating others into falsely accusing me—for instance, inmate Dawson was approached by Lee Merritz and A.W. Daniels, who asked him, 'Why are you protecting Lieutenant Jones?' Inmate Clowing was also asked the same question by Lee Merritz, and he approached inmate Warsaw, asking her, 'Why are you protecting Lieutenant Jones?' This information was provided to me by Inmate Brown, of her own free will."

CHAPTER 24

Diesel Therapy

The next day when I reported to work, Inmate Brown was in the Special Housing Unit—just as I had predicted. She had been admitted there pending an investigation. After about two months in the Special Housing Unit, she was sent to Perry, Florida, to the county jail, where she stayed for almost four months. Perry is the town where a couple of FBI agents were refused service at a restaurant because they were black. The waitress didn't know the men she turned down were F.B.I. agents.

I felt sorry for Inmate Brown; she didn't deserve that treatment. When she left Perry, she came back to FCI-Tallahassee, but only for a few minutes to board a bus headed to Texas. I received word that she looked broken down. Inmate Brown told one staff member that the institution had sent my picture to the county jail where she was being held and asked if I had visited her. The jail staff said they'd never seen me and that the only visitor was her son. The institution was still trying to take me down. They should have known I wouldn't break policy by visiting her. The SIA sure was a dumbass.

One of the lieutenants told Brown to keep her head up and continue fighting for justice. To this day, Inmate Brown has been in FMC-Fort Worth for six years, and her family has to travel 24 hours to visit her. Normally, an institution will try to locate you closer to home, but because Inmate Brown informed the institution about the captain's sexual advances, they were making her pay for it. She was transferred without an incident report, and in all my years in the Bureau of Prisons, I've never seen an instance where they transfer inmates that far from home without one.

I understand they had to get her away from the staff who had made sexual advances toward her, but they could have sent her to the Federal Prison Camp in nearby Marianna, Florida, or the Federal Prison Camp in Coleman, Florida. I contacted her congressman via email regarding Inmate Brown's case and even visited him when I was in Washington, D.C., but he didn't do anything about it. I understand he made an inquiry, but I'm sure they told him a lie. From time to time, I'd receive calls from Inmate Brown's family asking what they could do to get their loved one closer to home. I told them they would need to contact their congressman and continue reaching out to the regional director, urging them to look into the matter.

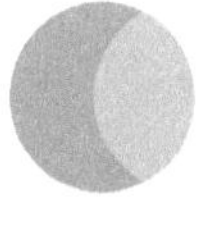

CHAPTER 25

I Took the Advice of My Doctor

When I had my next doctor's appointment, he asked if I was feeling okay. I told him, "No, I feel like hurting the people at the institution. I'm tired of their shit, and the only reason I haven't blown their brains out is that I have a family."

My doctor responded, "Garry, you can't keep living like this. You can't have those thoughts in your head."

"Man, if you worked where I worked, you'd feel the same," I said. "Doctor Bruce, I can guarantee you that one day someone is going to walk into that institution and blow someone's head off. Those people treat human lives like strings, wanting us to dance when they pull them. But I'm not the dancing type—I'm the kind of person who will beat your ass and think nothing of it. Every time I turn around, there's a damn bogus investigation on me, and the warden allows this bullshit. I regret having a family to care for; if I didn't, I'd have taken some people out by now—not with a weapon but with my bare hands. And if I get in trouble, I'll be the only one who suffers, not my family. Doctor Bruce, I'm getting to the point of no return. My depression is worsening, anxiety attacks are intensifying, and the only relief would come from going back into the institution to deal with those who've been agitating me."

"No, that's not the way, Garry," he said. "Let's revisit what I suggested three years ago—you should retire. I can't continue allowing you to come back to work with those thoughts in your mind. If you carry them out, I will be in trouble because I knew about them. Garry, I can put you back in the hospital, but when you get better and return to work, the job will trigger something in you and you may snap. Garry, it's up to you. I suggest you retire before you become an inmate, adding even more issues to your life. Please think about retirement."

"Okay, Doctor Bruce, I will call my grandmother and discuss it with her, and I'll let you know something next week," I said.

"Garry, I suggest you don't go back to work—it's not healthy," he added.

That night, I called my grandmother and told her what was going on. She agreed that I should retire. My grandmother understood I wasn't the type to hurt anyone unless they continued to mess with me—that's how she described it. She knew that if someone picked on me, I would do some serious damage. She must have sensed my frustration because she said, "Garry, I agree with the doctor; I think you should medically retire." Normally, my grandmother would tell me to persevere, but someone in the family must have informed her about the turmoil at my job.

My grandmother had never supported me quitting anything I'd started.

The following week, I returned to the doctor and told him my grandmother agreed with him. He instructed me to submit my retirement paperwork, and he would submit his recommendation as well. When I expressed my intent to retire, the warden called me to her office and said, "Garry, I received a call from the central office and was informed to put you on sick leave until your retirement paperwork goes through." I asked her when that would take place, and she said she didn't know.

"Since you don't know, I'll continue to work," I replied.

"I can't allow you to work, according to your doctor," she insisted, then made a phone call.

"Lieutenant Jones isn't sure he has enough sick time accrued to take this sick leave until retirement," she said. Moments later, the warden received another call stating she needed to place me in a less stressful environment until my paperwork was approved. I decided to go to the Detention Center to work in Receiving and Discharging (R&D). I could tell my retirement paperwork was likely to go through; they were clearly eager to get rid of me, but they still had something planned. If they knew I had enough sick leave, they would have demanded I not return to the institution.

A couple of months later, I was called in to work early. When I arrived, two agents awaited me in personnel. I asked what they wanted, and they tried to shake my hand again. I refused, stating, "Let's get down to business. What the hell do you want with me?"

One of the agents replied, "We're investigating you for failure to follow policy and procedures."

"What the hell did I do this time?" I asked.

"You went over to the Special Housing Unit and didn't sign in," the agent said.

"I don't know what you're talking about," I replied. "People go over to the Special Housing Unit all the time—sign in or forget to sign out. This is normal; emergencies happen, and you have to leave to handle them on the compound."

I picked up the phone and called the Special Housing Unit, speaking with Officer Ida. I asked if the captain, associate warden, and warden had made their rounds in Lock Up yet. She confirmed they had.

"Check the logbook and tell me who went over there without signing in or who forgot to sign out," I said.

She checked and said the captain, associate warden, and warden hadn't signed the book at all. I instructed Officer Ida to make a copy of that sign-out page and have the compound officer deliver it to me in personnel. When the officer arrived with the copies from the logbook, I showed them to the investigators and said, "You can say you have merit to the charges against me, but rest assured another EEO complaint will be filed if you don't charge the captain, associate warden, warden, and the rest of the staff who went over to the Special Housing Unit but either didn't sign in or forgot to sign out. This is selective prosecution and I'll report this to the Attorney General."

I had already hired a lawyer to file a lawsuit against the institution for discrimination. Before filing, my father made a profound statement. "Garry, paying a lawyer is a waste of time. The government has deep pockets compared to your one lawyer, who has to face off against ten government lawyers." I don't regret fighting the government, but I learned what my father meant.

My lawyer was lousy and sold me out. Before I paid him, he seemed excited about the case, but after getting my money, his enthusiasm evaporated as he claimed, 'This is going to be a hard case to win.' The truth is, he sold me out to the government. If I knew I wouldn't get in trouble for discussing what he'd done to me, I'd tell everyone in Florida that he's a sellout and put his name out there.

I was warned long ago to avoid hiring a lawyer in the same town as the one I was suing, because the judges' and lawyers' kids go to school together and are friends. But if you hire someone from a different town, the chances of them knowing the judge or other lawyers diminish, and they wouldn't feel conflicted because there's no connection.

When I returned to work a couple of hours later, I was summoned to the warden's office. She asked me to take a seat, which I did.

"Lieutenant Jones, your medical paperwork has been approved, and you don't have to report to work anymore. You are officially retired," she announced. "I'll work with personnel to prepare your file and they will inform you of the date and time for your retirement ceremony."

The warden attempted to make small talk, asking, "How long have you been working for the agency?"

I told her it had been 12 years.

"Have you ever worked for anyone else?" she inquired.

I responded that I'd been working since I was 16. "You had a pretty good work history," she noted, adding, "I noticed you were Correctional Officer of the Year in 1993. The agency will compensate you for your annual leave."

"What about my sick leave?" I asked.

"You know they can't pay you for your sick leave," she replied.

"I'm not leaving the government anything," I countered. "Actually, you can tell personnel to make my retirement effective until all my sick leave has been exhausted."

"Lieutenant Jones, you might as well forget about that sick leave," she said.

"I'm not leaving the government anything," I reiterated.

"Let me make a phone call," she said. "Lieutenant Jones, if we can convert your sick leave to annual leave, will that resolve the issue?"

I agreed.

She instructed me to head to personnel, where they would take my picture and issue my badge with credentials.

Rumors circulated through the institution that I was fired, explaining my long stay in the warden's office. I didn't feed into that nonsense when people began asking if I had been fired.

CHAPTER 26

Retirement Party

In August 2003, the institution threw me a retirement party. I wanted to leave quietly and told them I didn't want a celebration, but my friends Caldwell and Walkerfountaine insisted, "You deserve a party." Reluctantly, I went along with their advice.

When I arrived, some executive staff were present, along with my friends. The ceremony included two plaques and a clock, each engraved with "FCI-Tallahassee." Alcohol wasn't allowed on grounds, but some folks had drinks in their cars. A few people stood up to speak and roast me.

My friends said I had inspired them and wished I wouldn't leave. The party was enjoyable until the captain showed up with his daughter. He'd been told I didn't want him at the party, yet he still came, and bringing his daughter made it difficult for the staff to speak freely about me.

Happy Retirement

Retirement Cake

I noticed I hadn't seen Lieutenant Caldwell for a while and wondered where he was; of all my friends, he should have shared a few words. Lieutenant Walkerfountaine spoke up, saying, "G, Caldwell is outside because the captain is here, and you know how he feels about that guy. He won't come in until the captain leaves."

It was probably for the best that Caldwell stayed outside; given his feelings, he might've broken the captain's neck. Once the captain finally left, the party resumed. Caldwell returned and apologized, but I completely understood.

I received gifts of money, liquor, and cards—everything you could think of. My retirement cake was stunning, decorated with a picture of the institution and the words "God's Blessing Lt. Jones." Mrs. Minnefield from the Food Service Department had the inmates make the cake, and they outdid themselves. Everyone kept asking what my next move would be, and I told them I was relocating to Atlanta and planned to take it easy.

After the party, some friends came over to my apartment and drank beer from a keg. Now off institution grounds, they felt relaxed, and we wrapped things up around 3 a.m. After they left, I sat alone, drank more, and began reminiscing about the good times I had at the institution... I couldn't believe my career was over. On the flip side, had I not retired, I probably would have killed someone.

Hanging Retirement Chit – Career is Over

A couple of days later, Lieutenant Caldwell showed up with his truck and moved most of my belongings while I transported the rest in my car. I needed to find a place for my daughter to stay because she told me her mother was moving too. Just a week prior, my wife had asked me to talk to my daughter about not moving out and getting her own apartment until she stayed at home for a year. Latoya was attending Tallahassee Community College and was eager for her own space.

I had that conversation with my daughter, stressing the importance of staying home for now, considering she had ample time ahead to find a place. I was already under enough pressure, and with my wife leaving, the burden rested on me to come up with $800 for a deposit and one month's rent for Latoya.

My luck continued to worsen when the battery and alternator in my car died. This was the Lexus I'd given to Latoya because I wanted the better car for her to avoid breakdowns. I paid another $400 to get it fixed, which added up to $1,200 overall. I managed to move Latoya into her new apartment before leaving Tallahassee.

Finances were tight since I hadn't started receiving my retirement benefits. With the car finally fixed, I packed my things into my vehicle and went over to Caldwell's house, where he grilled ribs and we drank until we were full.

"Jones, you should stay in Tallahassee," Caldwell suggested, and I pondered it. If I'd known my wife was moving to Atlanta at the last moment, I would have told the apartment complex I was renewing my lease to stay in Tallahassee. The primary reason for my move was her presence in the city.

I called the apartment complex to see if I could get my old apartment back, but it was already rented, and there were no other one-bedroom options available. Having already made relocation plans, I decided to stick with them.

Moving To Atlanta

I left Lieutenant Caldwell's house late and got on Interstate 319 toward Thomasville, Georgia. Atlanta was roughly four and a half hours from Tallahassee. I took my time because I wanted to clear my head, contemplating: What am I going to do now that I'm young and retired? I had always worked hard; I loved my job, so how did I allow the government to destroy my health?

Most people would envy my situation—young and retired. Growing up, it was instilled in me to work hard and support my family. Though my wife and I were separated, I still had a responsibility to take care of my 12-year-old son. I knew I wouldn't earn the same amount in retirement, but that was no excuse to abandon my responsibilities. When you bring children into the world, it's your duty to care for them. It bothers me when people refuse to provide for their children.

I faced two major problems: one was my inability to work due to my deteriorating health, and the other was figuring out how to fill my abundant free time. I recalled my doctor saying before I left Tallahassee, "Garry, find something you enjoy, but don't do it enough to trigger another setback."

The more I went against my doctor's advice, the sicker I became. My illness was no joke; I had a tendency to push the limits. I loved beating the odds. Growing up, I dealt with asthma and ulcers but still played sports. It was hard to sit idle, yet I found myself struggling to cope with major depression and anxiety attacks. I had hidden this disease from everyone for thirty years. I prayed, fasted, and tried to keep busy with work and exercise, but the more agitated I became, the worse my condition worsened.

I realized I had to immerse myself in various activities; to truly live, I had to force myself to do so. Some days I felt like I was losing my mind. Devilish thoughts urged me to end my misery. The medication wasn't working—my doctor kept switching my prescriptions, searching for the right fit, but nothing helped. Alcohol was my only solace; I continued to self-medicate as it kept me alive.

I experimented with cocaine, but it made me paranoid over time. Marijuana was never an option because it always triggered paranoia for me. Being paranoid is akin to experiencing an anxiety attack, and I couldn't handle it. I recall being on the job, putting inmates on suicide watch because they couldn't cope with their depression. I often talked them down but secretly understood their pain.

I played the role of the strong one well; when I had suicidal thoughts on the job, nobody knew because I was always smiling— that was my front. Nobody would suspect the hell I was enduring. I watched a segment on TV one day before retiring, featuring a woman discussing her son's suicide; she never knew he was suffering from depression. She was devastated; her son left a note stating he couldn't bear the pain any longer. I connected deeply with that young man's struggle. I felt compelled to act.

I called a local TV station and inquired about the woman's interview. The show was called "It's Time," airing on Florida A&M University. The woman I spoke with recognized my desire to address the topic of depression. "The show you watched obviously affected you," she said.

"It did," I replied. I revealed my struggles with depression and expressed a desire to speak with the grieving mother, hoping to travel the country to raise awareness. I believed the issue wasn't receiving enough attention, given that 85 percent of those who suffer from depression commit suicide.

The woman invited me to join the show and discuss how depression affects me. Initially, I hesitated but ultimately agreed. She took down my information and promised to call me to set a time for the studio.

After hanging up, I thought, What have I done? Now inmates and staff will know what I'm dealing with and treat me differently. But another voice chimed in: This is a step towards healing.

I told my wife about the show, and she became furious.

"I don't know why you're going on TV to talk about your personal issues," she complained.

"Damn it, I'm trying to help people," I countered.

The night before I was set to tape the show, my wife called and asked if I was still going through with it. When I said yes, we argued again.

"I'm not embarrassed to talk about depression," I insisted. "That's why I'm sick now—holding back has only prolonged my healing. And you, as an evangelist, should want me to assist others." My wife was employed at Florida A&M University, and perhaps she didn't want her colleagues to know her husband struggled with depression. I was comfortable with who I was; I wasn't weak but battling a mind disease. The public often labels those suffering from depression as weak, but I disagree—that's why I didn't seek help more than thirty years ago.

The next day, my show was scheduled to tape at 2 p.m. I donned my suit and headed to the studio. Upon arrival, I spoke with the interviewer, who congratulated me for coming forward. "Most men hide their feelings, so your perspective as a lieutenant in the Federal Bureau of Prisons is significant, considering someone in your position typically wouldn't dare discuss this subject."

The show went well, and I was invited back for another episode, this time with a psychiatrist. The ratings soared. They asked me to return for a third episode, but I declined as I grew tired of discussing the topic. The nature of depression often leaves you feeling elated one day and utterly drained the next.

Years later, around November and December, people from Tallahassee called to inform me the show was airing again. I hoped someone watching would decide to seek help.

I finally arrived in Atlanta around 5 a.m. I called my cousin to let her know I was in her development. She came downstairs to open the door. Not unpacking, I went straight to the guest room and fell asleep.

When my cousin Ann got off work, I asked if she wanted something to drink. She declined, so I didn't mind drinking alone, though we had once enjoyed drinking together. I noticed she no longer drank as she used to.

By the week's end, I had consumed her bottle of Absolute Vodka, trying to figure out my next steps in Atlanta. I knew the city well and enjoyed being there. I felt no rush to do anything since it had become my home.

During the first year, I frequently found myself traveling to Tallahassee, North Carolina, and Washington, D.C. I realized I needed to do something meaningful with my life instead of wandering aimlessly. Some days, I drank to fill the void, while other days, I hit the highway, and at times, I isolated myself in my room for days on end. This behavior was unhealthy. I felt unstable and resisted seeing a doctor in Atlanta, despite knowing some of the nation's best were there. I felt more comfortable with my doctors in Tallahassee. Making changes can be challenging for anyone, but if you don't push through, you risk confining yourself and missing out on what the world has to offer.

CHAPTER 28

Traveling Man

In 2004, I made plenty of trips to North Carolina. During one of them, my uncle Jay asked, "What are you doing, Gold?"

"Nothing," I replied. "The doctor told me to find something I like doing, but the only thing I enjoy is Criminal Justice-type activities."

"Why don't you substitute in the school system two times a week?" he suggested. "This will help kill the boredom from retirement."

"Maybe I'll give it some consideration," I said, then added, "I'm thinking about creating an organization called Advocate4Justice to inform the world about the racial disparities in sentencing guidelines. Jay, there are a lot of people inside those walls—people who look like us."

He asked when I was going to D.C., and I said probably after I came back from Charlotte, N.C.

"Billy has tickets to the Carolina Panthers and the Washington Redskins," I explained. "But right now, I'm getting ready to go to the library and create myself an email because everyone keeps telling me I should get one so they can send me different material."

I hadn't used an email system in a long time. Later that evening, I went to the Neuse Library and asked the librarian how to create an email and how much it would cost. She told me to visit Yahoo and set up an account; it was free.

While trying to figure out how to create an email, I got frustrated because the librarian was taking so long to return to me. Then a little girl came over and said, "Sir, I can help you, but you have to register to get an email on Yahoo. You just need to fill out some questions on the page where it says 'Create a name and a password.'"

I went to that page and discovered I had to provide Yahoo with my life history before I could open an email account. I wondered if the government was requiring Yahoo to gather all this information about me. They definitely wanted to know my personal stuff. I complied with Yahoo's demands, and then the little girl asked, "Sir, what name do you want to use?"

It took me a minute to think of a name for my email account, and then my mind went to Advocate4Justice.

"Sir, that's a pretty name," the girl said.

"Thanks," I nodded.

"Go ahead and type in Advocate4Justice and create a password," she instructed.

When I typed in Advocate4Justice, I received a message saying that someone already had that name.

"Sir, you have to create another name," the girl advised.

"I don't want another name," I replied. "This one fits me."

I was getting really frustrated and said, "I'm going to try this one more time, and then I'm saying the hell with an email." I didn't even want one; my friend Maurice Parker was the one who suggested this email crap.

Then the librarian came over and remarked, "I see you've already started the process."

"Yes, thanks to this young lady," I replied.

The librarian rolled her eyes. I wasn't trying to be mean; I just was stating the truth—the girl was helping me. That comment hadn't been intended to insult the librarian.

I asked the young girl what year it was, and she said 2004. I typed in advocate4justice2004, and the computer accepted my name and password. I got kind of excited and thanked the little girl. I left the library and called Parker, saying, "I got an email—are you satisfied?"

"Yes, Jones, welcome to the new age. Now, when are you coming to D.C.?" he asked.

"Man, I don't know. Jay just asked me the same thing a couple of hours ago."

"When you come up to D.C., maybe you can talk with my kids about the criminal justice system," Parker suggested.

"Okay, but my daughter Latoya is beeping in, let me take her call," I said.

I asked my daughter how she was doing, and she said, "Dad, did you hear about Johnny Cochran?"

"No, what happened?"

"I heard on the news that he passed away."

"Toya, I didn't know he was sick," I said. "Let me call you back. I have Parker on the other line." I switched lines and told him about Cochran's death.

"Jones, are you for real?" he said.

"Yes, I'm for real," I replied. "I can guarantee you that the Goldmans and Nancy Grace are not disappointed."

"Why do you say that, Jones?"

"Because those folks are angry that O.J. Simpson was acquitted, and they hold Johnny Cochran accountable for just doing his job as an attorney," I explained. "They're not mad at O.J. Simpson's other lawyers. He had about four or five lawyers, but for some reason, people are mad at Johnny Cochran. Parker, I'm thinking about starting an organization. What do you think?"

"I think that's good, Jones. This will give you something to do," Parker replied. "Are you going to talk about what you discussed on TV in Tallahassee in 2003?"

"What shows are you talking about?"

"The show you went on where you discussed the disparity in sentencing guidelines concerning crack cocaine and powder cocaine," he reminded me.

"Parker, I forgot all about that show," I admitted. "I thought you were talking about the show on depression."

"Jones, you still haven't told me when you're coming to D.C.?"

"Man, I'm going to Charlotte to catch a Panthers game, and then I'm going to Tallahassee for a doctor's appointment and to visit my children, Latoya and Derrick," I said.

I spent a couple of days with my grandmother Tessie and then headed to Charlotte for the game. Afterward, I chatted with my friend Billy and my brother Pete before heading back to Atlanta. When I arrived in Atlanta, I got some sleep, and the next day I headed back to Tallahassee for my doctor's appointment.

CHAPTER 29

Post Traumatic Stress Disorder

While on my way to Tallahassee, I started thinking about the ribs that Lieutenant Caldwell was going to cook and the dinners Lieutenant Walkerfountaine and I were going to share. Walker can whip up some fine meals, and normally when I visit Tallahassee, my friends roll out the red carpet. They won't let me pay for food, gas, or a place to stay—these are true friends, to say the least.

I called my daughter Latoya and told her I'd be in town for a doctor's appointment and I'd probably stay for a week. Sometimes I go to Tallahassee for a couple of days, and it turns into a couple of weeks. I got a phone call from an organization asking if I was Lieutenant Jones, and I confirmed that I was.

"My name is Sue, and I've heard a lot about you," the woman said.

"What have you heard, Sue?"

"I heard that you advocate on behalf of incarcerated inmates," she replied.

"Sue, from time to time, I speak out, and every now and then someone wants to interview me about my views on crime," I said.

"Lieutenant Jones, do you mind giving us an interview?" she asked. "You've worked in the prison system, and you've been in the belly of the beast."

I asked her the name of her organization, and she said it was called the Coalition.

"We are located in Washington State," she told me.

I stayed on the phone with Sue for about an hour, then received a call from my doctor's office asking if I was still coming in for my appointment.

"I'm on the highway now, headed your way," I answered. "If nothing happens with traffic, I'll make it on time."

When I reached Tallahassee, I went straight to the doctor's office with about 30 minutes to spare. My doctor was glad to see me.

"Garry, are there any good doctors in Atlanta?" he asked.

"Yes," I replied, "but I don't like switching doctors, and besides, I have two children still here. When I know I'm coming to see them, I usually make an appointment with you."

"How does it feel to be retired?" he inquired.

"It feels the same to me, Dr. Bruce."

"What do you mean?"

"I mean I don't feel any different than I did when I was working," I said.

"How is your depression and anxiety coming along?"

"I still have them."

"With all the pressure lifted off you, you should be feeling a little better by now," he said.

"Well, I don't," I replied. "I still have racing thoughts. It would be better if I didn't have these dreams all the time."

"What dreams are you having?"

"Almost every night, I dream about the institution and how they retaliated against me."

"What do you see in those dreams?"

"I see myself coming to work in my uniform, going to the office, and the captain is always trying to set me up," I said. "I feel as though I'm still working. I wake up in a night sweat from time to time."

"I thought when you went to sleep, it was a chance to get away from your problems, not dream about them all the time," he replied.

"I could handle different dreams, but it's the same dream every night," I explained. "And if not every night, it's every other night."

"Garry, how long have you been having these dreams?"

"I was having them before I left the institution and after I retired."

"Why didn't you tell me about these dreams?"

"You didn't ask about them."

"But Garry, you felt the need to tell me now."

"Maybe I didn't think anything of the dreams, but now they're getting worse," I said.

Dr. Bruce closed his eyes for a moment and didn't say much. For a minute, I thought he might be asleep, but I knew that wasn't true. Once Dr. Bruce opened his eyes, he would always recite everything we talked about word for word.

"Garry, I want you to think about going to group therapy," he said.

"I don't want to think about going to any group therapy," I countered. "I don't want to hear about anyone's problems—I have enough of my own. Dr. Bruce, why can't I continue to have one-on-one conversations with you?"

"Garry, you are suffering from what we call PTSD—Post Traumatic Stress Disorder," he said.

"But Dr. Bruce, I've never been in the military," I argued. "How can I have that disorder? It's associated with military people who have been to war. I know I went to war every day inside those prison walls, but this wasn't the military."

"Garry, that's a misperception about PTSD," he explained. "You don't have to be in the military to experience it. You can have a traumatic experience, and it can affect you for a lifetime. There's no cure for this disorder, and that's why I want you to go to group therapy and continue taking your medication without allowing yourself to be stressed. What are you doing to kill time?"

"I'm trying to start an organization called Advocate4Justice," I said.

"What will this organization do?"

"It will inform people about the disparity in sentencing laws regarding crack and powder cocaine."

"That's great, Garry," he said. "I'm happy for you, but don't let yourself get stressed because you could easily have another setback. At the same time, I don't want you sitting around doing nothing."

"Well, Garry," he added, "it's time for me to see another patient. You need to think about group therapy in Atlanta."

"Okay, Dr. Bruce," I replied.

After leaving Dr. Bruce's office, I thought to myself, hell with some group therapy. Then I received another phone call from Washington, D.C.

"May I speak with Garry Jones?" the caller asked, and when I confirmed that was me, she said, "This is Linda from the OPM office."

"What do you want from me?" I inquired.

"Mr. Jones, have you started receiving Social Security disability yet?"

"No," I replied. "I thought you all said I would receive it a year after retiring?"

"No, Mr. Jones, this is not automatic," she explained. "You applied for it last year."

"It was denied," I said, "based on the fact that I was still on the Bureau of Prison payroll."

"Mr. Jones, we knew you were going to get denied, but when you submitted your paperwork for medical retirement, applying for Social Security disability was one of the requirements."

"Well, I did what you all asked me to do."

"Mr. Jones, you need to appeal."

"How long has it been since you applied for Social Security disability?" she asked.

"It's been over a year now."

"Mr. Jones, you need to apply for it again because the time for an appeal is 90 days."

"Okay, Linda, I will find a lawyer and apply for Social Security disability."

I hadn't been in Tallahassee for an hour, and I was already upset. I thought this trip would be nice. Latoya was in class, and Derrick was working. I called Walker at work and asked, "Did you leave the key under the door?"

She said yes. "I made spaghetti last night, and it's in the refrigerator with the garlic bread. Your liquor is in the cabinet, and your beer is in the bottom of the refrigerator. Big Daddy Caldwell brought the beer because he knew you were coming to town. He said he'll be over around 8 o'clock because he has to work the midnight shift."

"Thanks again, Walker," I said.

When I opened the door to Walker's house, I put my bags down and couldn't wait to dig into her spaghetti. I almost ate the whole pot.

When Walker came home, we popped some beer cans and shared a drink. We reminisced about old times, and before I knew it, Big Daddy was banging on the door in his uniform.

Big Daddy Caldwell always had to bend down when he opened the door. We chatted for a while, and before he left for work, he asked, "Jones, how long are you going to be in town?"

"I was planning on staying a week, but now it might just be a couple of days," I replied. "I spoke with OPM today, and they said I needed to apply for Social Security disability."

"Hell, I thought that shit was automatic when you retired with medical disability," he said.

"Go ahead to work," I said. "I'll talk with you in the morning, and we can go out for breakfast."

The next day, Caldwell came over to Walker's house, and we went out for breakfast. Afterwards, I called Latoya and told her I was coming over. She said she was home but had a class at 2 p.m.

I arrived at Latoya's apartment and asked her how her grades were, and she said they were great.

"Dad, have you seen Derrick yet?"

"No, but after I leave you, I'm going over to his apartment," I said.

"Dad, you know Derrick works at night," she reminded me.

"Damn, Latoya, I forgot about that," I admitted. "But maybe I can catch him now."

I called Derrick and asked if he was asleep. He said, "No, Pops, come on over."

I visited Derrick for a couple of hours and then headed back to Walker's house. When I got there, she was just coming into the complex. We walked into the house together, shared a drink, and talked. I told her I'd be leaving to go back to Atlanta in the morning, but once I returned, I'd have to find a lawyer to represent me for my Social Security disability case.

"I'm pissed because I received wrong information from the institution," I said. "It's been over a year, and I have to file for Social Security again. When I get back, I'm going to rest for about four weeks, and then I'll fly to Washington, D.C., to chill with Parker for a month. He has a friend at the college interested in doing all the paperwork for the organization."

"What organization are you talking about, G?"

"I'm trying to create an organization that will educate people about the laws and talk with kids about what will happen if they go the wrong way. Dr. Bruce told me to make sure I don't burn myself out—but I need to do something."

CHAPTER 30

I Wasn't Raised to Play by Their Rules

On my way back to Atlanta, I reflected on what Dr. Bruce had said. It weighed heavily on my mind. What had the government done to me? First, they exacerbated my depression and anxiety, and now this Post Traumatic Stress Disorder. How did I let them do this to me? Should I have overlooked the corruption and acted like most people—who, as long as it doesn't affect them, don't give a damn about anyone else?

This wasn't what I was taught growing up. My grandmother always fought for what she believed in. My Uncle Jay always said, "Do not let anyone take away your confidence."

In my opinion, those principles were solid. Even if I wanted to look the other way when I saw corruption, I couldn't—that's just not how I'm built. Sometimes I question God, as if to say, "Why did you make me this way? Why do I have to be the one who stands up for those people who see the same things I see but turn their heads? Why do I have to feel guilty when I don't correct what is wrong? Something has to give, God. If this is the work you have for me, you have to give me the energy and the desire to fight because I'm tired."

I would have plenty more moments when I questioned God. When I was growing up, we were taught not to question Him. I don't recall my grandmother ever teaching me this, but somehow I absorbed it.

When I arrived in Atlanta, I called a Social Security lawyer and shared my situation. He agreed to take the case and told me to keep all my doctor's appointments and not engage in any other activities. First and foremost, I was already doing that before I even called him, so why reiterate that I needed to keep my appointments and take my medication? This shit is not a game to me.

He told me not to do anything, while my doctor insisted I needed to actively do something to prevent going crazy. Hell, I wanted to engage in activities, even if it meant assisting the elderly at voting booths. The government had rigged this system so severely that if you played their game, you would end up dead—and that's what they ultimately want: for you to die without costing them a damn penny for all your hard work.

A couple of weeks later, I flew to Washington, D.C., to visit my friend Parker. He mentioned a woman who wanted to be part of the organization and who was willing to handle all the paperwork.

"Look, Parker, my organization isn't on a grand scale," I explained. "It's just something to keep me busy while disseminating some information. I need someone to run the organization because every other day, my mind changes about whether or not I want to keep it going."

The lady Parker introduced me to was Mrs. Hayday, a woman in her 70s with plenty of ideas for the organization. She even convinced me to get a website. I told her I didn't know how to create one.

"I can't do anything that's going to drive me crazy," I said. "I don't work on computers that much, and who is going to maintain the website?"

"We will find someone to do it," she assured me. Then I suggested Sue, the woman who had called me from Washington State.

"Her organization does things like this," I stated.

Hayday called Sue, who replied, "We'd be happy to build him a website. Just tell us what he wants on it, and we will maintain it."

I began getting excited about having a website. Since it was mine, I wanted to be involved in the planning stage and influence its appearance. I envisioned my African heritage as the background, using the colors of Kente cloth.

Mrs. Hayday began looking at different websites to see how she wanted the URLs to look.

"It doesn't matter, just make sure I have Kente cloth in the background," I said.

It was strange how one day I could be excited about the website and the next day, I couldn't care less about it—or the organization. My mood swings would rise and fall intermittently. I eventually stepped back from the website equation, letting Sue and Mrs. Hayday handle all the technical details.

For the next few days, Parker was busy preparing his college seminar, and I was one of the guest speakers. On the day of the seminar, Parker reminded me not to exceed five minutes, to which I replied that I didn't know how I could teach the students anything in that short time frame.

"Jones, we have a timeline," he insisted.

"Damn it, Parker, what kind of guest speaker am I supposed to be with only five minutes to speak?"

When it was my turn, I ended up speaking for about ten minutes. It was evident that the students, parents, and professors were intrigued by my words.

After staying with Parker for a couple of weeks, I flew back to Atlanta. It was January 2005, and I wanted to participate in the Rev. Dr. Martin Luther King celebration. I got up that morning and went to Ebenezer Baptist Church to hear some inspiring speakers. I love listening to articulate speakers, especially the late Martin Luther King Jr., Malcolm X, Minister Farrakhan, and now President Barack Obama.

When I arrived at the church, several speakers took the podium, including Dr. King's children and their mother, Coretta Scott King. I remember Rev. Joseph Lowery mentioning that President George W. Bush would be coming to lay a wreath at Martin Luther King's gravesite, and that the president's entourage was on the way down Auburn Street. He noted that Bush had only made the last-minute decision to come and hadn't notified them until late, which forced them to alter their plans. Lowery wasn't thrilled about this—it meant everyone would have to exit the church through the back door. The only reason the president came to lay a wreath was because he was in town for a fundraiser, and since he was already here, he saw fit to pay a visit.

A couple of months earlier, Bush had made a controversial statement about how race should play a part in college admission, triggering an uproar across the country. Now he had the nerve to want to lay a wreath on Dr. King's gravesite. Martin Luther King advocated for unity across races, while President Bush seemed to be tearing them apart. It was hypocritical for him to show up.

Rev. Lowery urged anyone who wanted to object to Bush's presence to go across the street and protest. What was supposed to be a small protest transformed into a large gathering. TV cameras flooded the scene, and somehow I found myself grabbing a bullhorn. Once Bush's entourage approached, the city of Atlanta used local buses to separate the crowd from Martin Luther King's gravesite.

As Bush got closer, I yelled through the bullhorn, "Where is the weapon of mass destruction?" I instructed the crowd to chant, "Bush is the weapon of mass destruction." They followed my lead, repeating, "Where is the weapon of mass destruction? Bush is the weapon of mass destruction. Go home, Bush, go home."

I was aware of government agents on the rooftops of tall buildings with guns; some agents were clearly visible. I knew there were undercover agents in the crowd pretending to protest. I wasn't naive; I had been in law enforcement my entire life. It's the unseen agents that frighten me.

The protest escalated quickly. A few people were arrested, and police attempted to control the crowd, but chaos ensued. I instructed people to hold hands and bend down if they had to, but to avoid actions that would land them in jail. I wanted the protest to remain peaceful—I wasn't into rowdy protests. Those don't effectively get your point across; the police are just waiting for an opportunity to crack down. Some teenagers were trying to topple the buses, and I urged them to stop, but they wouldn't listen.

The police managed to infiltrate the crowd and apprehend a few people. They had their sights set on me; they recognized that with my suit, I wasn't trying to instigate trouble. I never imagined I'd be involved in a protest when I left the house that day.

When the protest concluded, I returned home feeling drained. Before reaching my house, I called Pizza Hut and ordered a pepperoni and sausage pizza. When I exited the shop, my cousins Ann and Sarah drove up and asked, "Where have you been, all dressed up?"

I told them I'd attended the King celebration, but they had no idea what had transpired. Later that night, while I was in bed, Ann came to my room and said, "Gold, you are on TV."

Goldwater is my nickname, but Ann calls me Gold.

When I got up to check the TV, the news report on the protest had already ended, though I did see myself on CNN the next day. They aired a clip of me protesting.

The following day, I received a call from Mrs. Hayday asking me to send some pictures of myself to feature on my website, along with my bio.

I had heard about a march scheduled for August 2005 in front of the White House, organized by another activist. It was titled the Millions More March for Incarcerated Inmates, aimed at raising awareness of the staggering number of incarcerated individuals in the United States.

I contacted the woman responsible for organizing the march and expressed my desire to participate. She replied, "I will add your website and your name to the list of speakers."

On August 13, 2005, in blistering temperatures soaring to 100 degrees, I delivered a ten-minute speech addressing the racial disparity in sentencing guidelines between crack cocaine and powder cocaine. The crowd roared in response. Somehow, my message resonated with them; they felt me, and I could feel them.

When I stepped off the podium, Fox News sought to interview me about my involvement with an organization called LEAP, which stands for Law Enforcement Against Prohibition. Founded on March 16, 2002, LEAP comprises current and former law enforcement officials who believe the nation's existing drug policies have failed to achieve their intended goals of addressing crime, drug abuse, addiction, juvenile drug use, and the illegal drug trade.

Talking to the Media on War on Drugs – Fox News

Speakers and Featured Participants

From *Drug Truth Network*: Journey For Justice On-site Coverage, August, 2005 (mP3 audio): Part 1 - Part 2 -

Bryan Stevenson, of the Equal Justice Inittative, will discuss Criminal Justice Sentencing. Mr. Stevenson, Executive Director of EJI and Professor of Clinical Law at New York University School of Law, has won national acclaim for his work challenging bias against the poor and people of color in the criminal justice system.

Since graduating from Harvard Law School and the Harvard School of Government, Stevenson has assisted in securing relief for dozens of condemned prisoners, advocated for poor people, and developed community-based reform litigation aimed at improving the administration of criminal justice.

Garry L. Jones, the Advocate4Justice, is a motivational speaker who has made guest appearances on local television in Tallahassee, Fl., among others. A retired Lieutenant for the Federal Bureau of Prisons, he now speaks out for people adversely affected by the failed war on drugs. Garry has recently joined the Speaker's Bureau of LEAP (Law Enforcement Against Prohibition)

"During my career as a Correctional Officer, I would often ask myself the question: Why is the largest percentage of inmates black, when blacks in the United States are only 13% of the population? Why is prison so black when 80% of people in this country are white?

"When I retired in 2003, it became obvious that there had to be a way to advocate for justice for all people. Today, I am that advocate who is standing up and speaking out on behalf of thousands of prisoners who have been affected by mandatory guideline sentencing. I hope you will join our growing network of others working to end drug war injustice."

By waging a war on drugs, the government has only aggravated these societal problems—making them far worse. We believed a system of regulation, rather than prohibition, is a less harmful, more ethical, and more effective public policy.

I told reporters we should legalize drugs and allow the government to control and tax them. The majority of the people incarcerated in America are there for drug offenses, which is crippling the economy; it costs taxpayers $55 billion a year to house inmates. The war on drugs is a joke: the government spends $69 billion annually to fight it, yet drugs are more plentiful and cheaper than ever before.

We need to build more drug rehabilitation centers instead of more prisons. The main reason I support legalizing drugs is that this would reduce the violence associated with dealing. A long time ago, alcohol was illegal, and the government resisted legalizing its sale. Ultimately, they had no choice because the violence and corruption linked to rum running were too significant to ignore.

Law enforcement also becomes corrupt. I worked in law enforcement and witnessed firsthand the corruption of officers bringing drugs into prisons for extra money—much more than their annual salary. Sometimes, when police stop someone with a large amount of drugs, they are easily influenced to turn a blind eye, especially when offered $50,000 to look the other way.

The same corruption is happening at the border. I have a friend in border patrol who told me, "Lieutenant Jones, if I were crooked, I could get rich by letting in people who smuggle drugs from Mexico to the United States." The agents are profiting by allowing illegal immigrants to cross the border with drugs—and being paid handsomely for it.

If the United States were genuinely serious about the war on drugs, my perspective would be entirely different. We have been fighting this war for far too long without seeing any results. The U.S. gives Mexico roughly $20 billion a year to help combat the drug war, but it's unclear whether this money is meant to curb drug trafficking or deter illegal immigration. Either way, it's not working; things have only gotten worse.

If the U.S. truly wanted to stop illegal immigration and drug trafficking, it should close all borders instead of just some. I believe alcohol is the worst drug ever legalized; deaths from drunk driving are far too common. I haven't found statistics on deaths from marijuana overdose, while cigarettes, although legal, rank high in mortality.

I don't condone the use of any drug for recreational purposes. The harsh reality is that many kids today look up to drug dealers and cartels. Some young people shun grocery store or fast-food jobs, believing they can earn in an hour selling drugs what others make in a week. They might prioritize bling over education, thinking the quickest way to flashy cars and extravagant homes is through drug sales. One reason drug dealers carry guns is to protect their territory. If drugs were legalized, who would the cartels recruit? This could put them out of business since there would no longer be a need for violent territory disputes.

We can rebuild our neighborhoods. If drugs are legalized and government-regulated, it may take a few years to see a difference, but I can guarantee crime will decline. Can you imagine how people felt when the government announced it would legalize alcohol again by repealing Prohibition? Many thought the government had lost its damn mind. Some may think I'm crazy for supporting this idea. When I joined LEAP, I expressed my belief: "U.S. drug laws have unjustly targeted and weakened the African American community."

I witnessed the futility of the war on drugs firsthand, retiring as a senior lieutenant after a 16-year career in our state and federal prison systems. "How can we hope to keep drugs out of our schools if we can't keep drugs out of maximum-security prisons?" I asked.

I became a LEAP speaker to support alternative policies that would reduce death, disease, crime, and addiction—four categories exacerbated by the war on drugs. When I spoke for LEAP, I made that argument and presented facts about what was really happening.

Fact: Did you know we spend $69 billion a year fighting the war on drugs? If we're spending that much, why is the government cutting back on funding for law enforcement, including police, corrections, and border patrol jobs? Shouldn't they be giving law enforcement everything it needs to tackle the drug war?

Fact: The first round of mandatory minimum sentencing was enacted in 1951, and it was repealed with bipartisan support 20 years later. Guess who backed the repeal? Yep, George H.W. Bush, then a congressman from Texas. With his son now in the White House, it would be a great time for history to repeat itself.

Fact: In 1969, President Richard Nixon called for the war on drugs and established mandatory minimum sentencing. Sixteen years later, it was shown to be ineffective, almost bankrupting the country, while the drug problem persisted and worsened.

Fact: On June 19, 1986, an election year, Len Bias, a basketball star selected by the Boston Celtics, died of a cocaine overdose. Not a crack cocaine overdose—cocaine.

Fact: After Bias's death in 1986, Democrats in Congress seized a political opportunity to outflank Republicans by getting tough on drugs. During the 1984 election, Republicans successfully accused Democrats of being soft on crime. House Speaker Tip O'Neill, whose constituents were appalled by Bias's death, recognized the power of an anti-drug campaign and pursued it.

Fact: By 2006, 20 years after Len Bias's death, there were still more drugs entering the U.S. The drugs were cheaper, and we hadn't made a dent in stopping them. The only thing the U.S. is doing is locking people up and throwing away the key. If the U.S. wants to end the war on drugs, why are they still funding Mexico and South America, where most drugs originate? The drug war isn't about Len Bias; it's about incarcerating minorities, keeping them in prison for long periods to manufacture products for companies like Victoria's Secret, Boeing, and Eddie Bauer. These companies subcontract with firms that use low-cost prison labor to produce everything from aircraft components to lingerie and software packages.

In Nevada, prisoners make waterbeds for Vinyl Products, Inc. Another company, Labor to Industry (formerly Lockhart Technologies), employs 60 Texas prisoners to create electronic circuit boards. The Washington Marketing Group hires prisoners as telemarketers, while South Carolina Cap and Gown, Inc. has prisoners making graduation gowns.

Fact: From 1954 to 1976, the Federal Bureau of Prisons' population increased from 20,000 to 24,000. By 1986, the Bureau was incarcerating 36,000 inmates. Twenty years later, that number skyrocketed to more than 190,000 inmates. More than half of that population consists of drug offenders, most serving sentences established in the weeks following Len Bias's death.

Garry Jones, Founder of Advocate4justice speaking for the organization L.E.A.P. about the unjust racist mandatory minimum sentencing laws that increased the prison population.

There is much more to this story. Major corporations benefit from prison labor. Are you wondering why you don't have a job or why you're getting laid off? I'll tell you the reason: Inmates are taking your jobs, and you—Americans who haven't committed any crimes—are getting the short end of the stick.

I want you to know that the Federal Bureau of Prisons is using inmates as operators for various types of information that civilians need. You know what I mean—"City and State, please." Those are inmates you're talking to. The Federal Correctional Institution in Tallahassee, Florida, and the Federal Correctional Institution at Butner, N.C., are employing inmates as phone operators. The Federal Correctional Institution in Memphis, Tennessee, has inmates making sensors that go on our bombs. Have you wondered why those bombs are not hitting their targets?

Before you complain that a non-violent offender should stay in prison for life, think about the jobs they are taking from the public. I agree we should have prisons, and some people do need to spend a long time there. But the prisons are primarily filling up with non-violent offenders serving 15 years to life. Meanwhile, violent offenders for rape, child molestation, murder, and spousal abuse are getting out before non-violent offenders.

I became the Advocate4Justice because, after years of witnessing these unfair laws while working in the Federal Bureau of Prisons, I decided to start an organization that promotes change and brings balance to the criminal justice system—hence the birth of Advocate4Justice. I began speaking to legislators about the need to reinstate federal parole in the Federal Prison System.

In early September 2005, I received a call from Jessie Jason's brother, Noah Robinson, asking if I could speak on behalf of inmates at the Congressional Black Caucus Conference. Noah arranged for all my expenses to be covered by his wife, Alfreda Robinson—who I call Free.

Speaking On Critical Topics Around the Criminal Justice System

Noah is serving three life sentences for conspiracy, and I personally believe he's innocent. I spoke at the conference, but there were so many organizations there that I only got four minutes. The crowd received my message well, but Congress wasn't getting the picture. They created these bad laws, and it was time for them to change. Sadly, Congress makes the mistake of sticking with what's popular instead of what's right.

In November 2005, an organization elected not to attend a Drug Conference in Long Beach, California, and called me to ask if I could go instead. I agreed. All fees were covered to fly to California and attend different sessions during the conference. LEAP also asked if I would be attending and said they would pay for the hotel and meals.

This was great for me, but I could feel myself getting burned out—and the thought of what my doctor had warned me about began to weigh on my mind. While at the conference, an overseas television station started interviewing some members of LEAP, and our coordinator asked me to join the interview.

I wasn't a robot, and LEAP knew that. They understood that whatever I said came from the heart. If I didn't believe it, I wouldn't speak it. One thing I appreciate about this organization is they agreed I could also talk about my own organization. Sometimes I got stares when I mentioned LEAP, but the truth is the truth.

My organization's mission is to bring balance to the federal criminal justice system by giving non-violent offenders a second chance at life and freedom. Advocate4Justice strives to do our part in educating society about relevant issues that affect our country; to end racial injustice; to reinstate federal parole (made retroactive); to end the abuse of conspiracy laws; and to urge the President of the United States to use his power to grant executive clemencies.

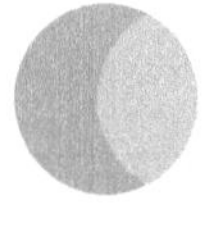

CHAPTER 31

The Killings at F.C.I. Tallahassee Could Have Been Avoided

One summer morning, I took my cousin Sarah to a dental appointment. While heading there, my cell phone rang off the hook. Friends from the Federal Correctional Institution-Tallahassee were calling to tell me what had happened inside the detention center. They informed me that one officer had been killed, along with an Internal Affairs agent. They also said one of the lieutenants who used to stay beside me had been shot as well. It was all over CNN.

I must admit I wasn't surprised. I later found out the reason this happened was that officers were being arrested for a misdemeanor charge of having sex with inmates and bringing in contraband. Yes, all involved were black officers—except for one who claimed to be Native American when it benefited him.

A couple of days earlier, one white officer was allowed by the administration to resign. This was Tallahassee's way of doing things—arrest black staff while letting white employees resign, even when both were having sex with inmates. The lieutenant who got shot and survived had worked in the Special Investigation Office, which contributes to these investigations. I can imagine he had a big smirk on his face when he was walking inside with the agents to arrest the officer, but later that smirk probably turned into a groan as he lay on the floor, fearing death.

I wasn't surprised when the warden claimed she didn't know what was going on. Every warden is expected to know when agents are coming into the institution to make arrests—she should have been the first to be notified. The fact that Special Investigation Agent Lee Merritz always seemed to circumvent the system and that the warden was clueless meant he was allowed to get away with a lot.

The warden stated that she thought a training exercise was taking place; even if this were true, someone should have informed her. Nothing goes on in that institution without notifying the warden.

The warden claimed she heard gunshots and thought they were firecrackers. How in the hell can you not know a major arrest is about to happen at your institution when the Tallahassee Police Department and Internal Affairs are present?

I also learned that arrest warrants were issued the previous evening. Once the warrants were issued, they should have been sent to the officers' homes for the arrests—rather than waiting for the officers to arrive for work the next morning to grandstand in front of everyone. Lives could have been saved.

The staff who witnessed this tragedy were now suffering from Post-Traumatic Stress Disorder. Can you imagine coming into work and seeing your fellow coworkers riddled with bullets? More than 30 shots were fired at that officer, and the agent who died was shot by other law enforcement officers. This entire tragedy was one big screw-up. The officers involved were sentenced to at least one year in prison—except for the white officer, who was said to have suffered a mild stroke. This doesn't have a damn thing to do with his avoiding prison. I've worked in six different prisons and processed inmates with all types of ailments. The only reason that officer didn't go to prison was that he was white.

One day, I received a call from a reporter from the *Saint Petersburg Times*. "Mr. Jones, I was told to call you because you were a lieutenant at F.C.I. Tallahassee, and maybe you could shed some insight on the recent shooting," she asked. "Do you think this incident could have been avoided?"

I talked to her for about two hours while visiting my grandmother in North Carolina. This reporter was the only one I spoke with who had the guts to print all the truth. However, when the article came out, she only included two lines about what I had said, referring to me as a retired correctional officer instead of a retired lieutenant. She listed other employees who were lieutenants simply as "lieutenants."

This makes me wonder if she checked my credentials. Did the institution list me as a retired correctional officer, or was it just a slip of the pen? While I'm not a huge fan of titles, I did retire as a lieutenant—not an officer, and my retirement badge clearly states "Retired Lieutenant."

Nevertheless, she wrote a powerful article exposing everything that went on in the institution. This lady was brave. I was also interviewed by a reporter from the *Tallahassee Democrat*.

She came to see me in Atlanta and we spoke for several hours. I provided her with more than 50 documents. Unfortunately, her supervisor refused to allow her to print the article. The corruption in Tallahassee has always been saved by the bell.

I'm Retired, but the Government is Still Retaliating Against Me

In August 2006, I flew to New York for a LEAP event in Times Square. I had already decided I no longer had the desire to advocate for anything; my depression and anxiety were worsening. I was ready to listen to the doctors and stop trying to juggle too many activities, but in reality, I wasn't doing much at all. My depression would be present regardless of my activities, and I was still taking my medication as directed—to no avail. My doctor frequently adjusted my dosage and switched my medication. Despite being a regular attendee at group therapy, I wasn't seeing results and wasn't feeling any better.

A couple of days before my scheduled New York visit, my mother called to tell me my aunt Arnetta's condition was worsening, and I might need to come to Maryland to see her. While I planned to visit her after returning to Atlanta, the urgency in my mother's voice indicated that my aunt didn't have much time left.

I called my sister Alicia, who lives in New York, and asked if she could pick me up at my hotel, where I could stay with her while deciding whether to drive to Maryland afterward.

Alicia cooked chicken, collard greens, and potatoes when I arrived at her place. I was surprised—previously, she had always ordered takeout. Acknowledging my struggle with depression and anxiety, Alicia was a good listener. We had a heart-to-heart, and I asked if she could arrange for me to take the Amtrak train to visit my aunt. Facing my aunt's impending death was something I didn't want to confront. The next morning, Alicia took me to the train station, gave me a few dollars, and I boarded the train straight to Maryland.

When I arrived, my friend Maurice Parker was waiting for me. We headed directly to the hospital to visit my aunt, who was pleasantly surprised to see me and asked how long I would be in town. I told her I'd stay until her last breath.

"You're about to make me cry," she said.

I reassured her she could cry, explaining how much I loved her and how lost I would feel when she passed. Tears rolled down our cheeks, and then she drifted back to sleep.

Six weeks later, my aunt passed away. I had kept my promise to be by her side every day. I felt devastated because, whether you know someone is going to die or their death catches you completely by surprise, it always breaks your heart. I've loved all my aunts and uncles—and they've loved me.

After the funeral, I returned to Atlanta. A few days later, one of the activists asked if I still planned to go to Alabama to speak at her event. I wanted to say no, but I had given her my word. I managed to attend, but I wasn't feeling well when I arrived. Before I spoke, she introduced me as someone who "travels around the world to speak." She really hyped me up. That statement would haunt me later. I spoke for about five minutes and then returned to Atlanta.

I wasn't paid for this, although it was never about the money for me; it was about educating the public on what was happening within the prison system and the bad laws Congress had created. The very thing I had loved most was the same thing I had come to hate. I no longer desired to speak publicly and didn't again until the president of the Brotherhood Ministry at my church asked if I could address the youth. I reluctantly agreed.

In 2007, I filed for divorce from my wife. Around that time, my Social Security case finally went before a judge, three and a half years after my initial application. In May 2007, I appeared at the Atlanta Courthouse and spoke with an administrative law judge via satellite. My lawyer spoke first, followed by the judge, who then asked me a couple of questions.

She inquired how I was feeling, and I replied that I wasn't well mentally. When asked what was going on, I explained that I was still suffering from depression and anxiety, as well as having nightmares. She asked if I was hearing voices, and I said no. "I know you have an organization called Advocate4Justice, as well as a website," she said, describing its contents. She asked if I had been to California, and I replied affirmatively. "Did you speak to a television station while you were there?" she asked, and I confirmed.

The judge knew everything on my website. I hadn't hidden anything before the court. Some people suggested I should act crazy in front of the judge, but I wasn't going to do that—I was simply suffering from a mental illness.

"Mr. Jones, do you still speak to groups?" She asked. "No, I don't have the desire to speak," I answered. When she asked why, I explained that my depression and anxiety were worsening. "Mr. Jones, do you take your medication?" she inquired. "Yes, Your Honor."

"Mr. Jones, who manages your website?"

"An organization out of Washington State, Your Honor," I said. "I don't know how to do any of that technical stuff."

"Mr. Jones, I see you often speak about mandatory sentencing laws," she noted. "Yes, Your Honor."

I don't recall every question she asked, but I told her I was handing many responsibilities over to my brother because I couldn't handle the stress. I explained that I have volunteers in my organization against mandatory minimum sentencing laws related to crack and powder cocaine, doing much of the work.

"Mr. Jones, you mentioned the medication makes you lethargic?" "Yes, Your Honor."

"Do you drive out of town, Mr. Jones?" I said I did. "How can you drive when the medication makes you lethargic?"

"Your Honor, when I travel, I don't take my medication until I reach my destination. Sometimes my relatives drive out of town, and I ride with them."

I was honest; I told the judge the reason I started my organization was that my doctor wanted me occupied with something I liked instead of sitting around doing nothing.

After the hearing, I returned home. Two weeks later, my attorney called to inform me my Social Security disability had been approved.

"I don't believe anything until I see it in writing," I replied. A couple of weeks later, I found out it was true. My disability had been approved, and I would receive both back pay and a monthly check. Since he was under 18, my son would also receive back pay and a monthly check. I knew the Office of Personnel Management would deduct my back pay because they had been paying my pension while I was out of work.

My organization wrote two additional letters on behalf of inmates—one to President Bush and another to the Inspector General's office, exposing ongoing corruption.

Those letters were written in July, alongside another informing inmates that my health was deteriorating and that I could no longer advocate for them.

I began to wonder why it took so long for my checks to start arriving. In September 2007, I received a letter from the administrative law judge overseeing my case, stating she had rescinded her favorable decision, reverting it to an unfavorable ruling based on a videotape and four anonymous witnesses who provided testimony to the Office of Inspector General. I was devastated. I reached out to my attorney, who couldn't believe it.

My attorney wrote the judge, requesting another hearing and asking to subpoena the investigating officer and those four anonymous witnesses.

The judge responded that she had reviewed my attorney's letter and was arranging a time for a video teleconference hearing. However, she denied the request to subpoena the investigator and witnesses, stating she didn't find it necessary for a full and fair inquiry into the matter. She claimed she would provide me with the names of the witnesses referenced in the report by the hearing date. But needless to say, she never provided me with the names of the witnesses or evidence against me. This was a violation of my constitutional rights—she violated my Sixth Amendment rights by not allowing me to face my accusers.

On December 13, 2007, I went back to court and faced the same judge over video teleconference. My lawyer spoke, providing the judge with letters from LEAP stating that they had paid my travel expenses, such as lodging, transportation, and meals. The letter also clarified that they weren't compensating me to speak.

Another letter from a different organization explained that they maintained my website and made all necessary changes because I didn't know how to do it myself.

A letter was written on my behalf stating that I wasn't paid to speak in Alabama at a rally. The letter noted that the introduction labeling me as someone who traveled around the world was intended to hype the crowd and attract attention.

After my attorney laid out the facts, the judge wanted to speak with me.

"Good morning, Mr. Jones; how are you feeling?"

"I'm not feeling well, Your Honor. In fact, I feel worse than I did when we met in May 2007."

"Mr. Jones, we received a videotape from a rally in Alabama where you were introduced as someone who speaks around the world."

"That's true, Your Honor; the lady who introduced me did say that, but it was intended to energize the crowd," I replied.

Speaking in Montgomery, Ala. for the National Day of
Justice held in every state.

"Your Honor, this rally was held in 2006 before my first hearing with you, and that footage was posted on my website. I assumed you reviewed everything on my website based on the questions you asked."

"Mr. Jones, do you attend counseling through your church?"

"Yes, Your Honor," I said. "I also participate in my group sessions. I need to walk to lose weight because I have chronic kidney disease." Additionally, I said, "Your Honor, I will continue going to church; that's where I receive my spiritual healing."

"Mr. Jones, have you been inside a gym since 2003?"

"Yes, Your Honor, I have, but I can't work out anymore due to arthritis in my shoulders."

"Mr. Jones, do you travel to North Carolina?"

"Yes, Your Honor; I travel to North Carolina to visit relatives for family reunions, weddings, and funerals."

The judge didn't mention anything about the anonymous letter dated February 2007, which she had received. The only thing my organization did in February 2007 was send a newsletter to inmates, but that was all done before my first hearing.

If she had asked about this during the first hearing, I would have explained. At a hearing, you can't remember every detail unless someone prompts you.

After the judge finished with my hearing, she asked her vocational rehabilitation expert if I could fold clothes, among other odd questions. He confirmed that I could. The vocational rehabilitation expert went on to describe to the judge how many jobs were available for me.

My attorney questioned the vocational rehabilitation expert about whether he had read my medical records, to which he replied no. My attorney insisted he review my medical records, and after doing so, asked, "Do you think he can go back to work?" The vocational expert said no.

The judge concluded the hearing and said she would make a decision within 30 days.

After the hearing, my attorney concluded that my case was political. On February 4, 2008, the judge still denied my claim. My attorney didn't handle appeals and recommended several lawyers who would. I tried to contact five additional lawyers, but none would take the case.

A few lawyers claimed they had never heard of a judge ruling fully in favor of a Social Security case and then rescinding her decision. They'd heard rumors of cases like mine occasionally, but that was it. The next step was to appeal to the Appeals Office in Falls Church, Virginia. In May 2008, they refused to review my case. By June 2008, my only option was to appeal to Federal Court. Vikki Hankins, vice president of the Advocate4Justice organization, wrote the appeal because no attorney would take the case.

I spoke with someone at the Atlanta Social Security Office, who instructed me to send a copy of the Civil Action for Court Review to their office, and they would forward the paperwork to the U.S. District Court for the Northern District of Georgia, Atlanta division. I was told the filing fee would be waived.

I haven't heard back from the Atlanta Social Security Office, despite sending the documents certified with a return receipt on July 8, 2008. That same month, I also filed a lawsuit against the Social Security Office for violating my civil rights. As of today, my lawsuit is still pending. Will I win my case? I don't know, but I encourage everyone who has ever filed for Social Security disability to keep fighting.

The Woman Who Taught Me Integrity and Principles Passed Away

It was January 15, 2009, a Thursday morning, and I felt refreshed. The day before, our church had participated in a 12-hour fast. I couldn't wait to get into the basement to work out. I remember it vividly: I was at the top of the stairs, talking to my cousin, who waited at the bottom to leave for work. The next thing I knew, I was tumbling down the steps, losing all control of my body; it felt like a dream, but it was reality.

The pain was unbearable, and I couldn't recall what had happened. All I knew was that I'd never felt such agony in my life. My cousin asked what happened, and I told her I didn't know; she needed to tell me.

She said I must have passed out and asked if I was okay. I assured her I would be fine, but the pain was so intense that

I asked her to get me a trash can because I felt nauseous. My cousin insisted on calling an ambulance, but I convinced her I was fine, even though I knew I wasn't. I had never experienced such excruciating pain, but I dismissed it and told her to go to work. If things got worse, I reasoned, I would drive myself to the doctor.

My cousin, Ann, noticed my elbows had swollen like balloons and that I was limping from a bruised hip. I thought to myself, please go to work, because if you don't, I'm going to burst into tears. She could see I wasn't okay, and I finally let her take me to a local orthopedic physician. I recognized I was injured but underestimated how bad it was.

Upon arriving at the doctor's office, I learned he wasn't in, so I had to see an interim physician. After the usual formalities, a hundred questions, and 16 x-rays later, the results showed I only had a contusion on my hip. He said he wanted to see me back on Monday, but I told him I was going to the inauguration and needed pain medication. He advised against traveling but that wasn't what I wanted to hear; I was determined to witness history as the first black president was sworn in. I had planned for this moment, and no one was going to stop me.

Once home, I got into bed, and my cousin opted to work from home instead of going to the office. She worried about me. She made me stay in bed because she knew I would be tempted to go up and down the stairs, and my fall must have terrified her. The more time I spent in bed, the more I realized something was off with both my elbows. They felt tight, and the pain was unbearable; I played it off when my cousin inquired about my well-being.

The next morning, I heard a knock at my bedroom door; it was my cousin asking how I felt. She had just received a call from North Carolina, and my family wanted to know if I was still alive. I finally admitted that I wasn't feeling good and told her to go about her day. I decided not to go to the inauguration and promised to see the doctor if things worsened. After she left, I found I couldn't move my elbows without tears streaming down my face. I popped three pain pills and took a shower.

Then something came over me. I had promised my grandmother I would make it to the inauguration, and I'd told the people who read my book, "Straight Out of Hell: The True Character of a Man," that I would see them in D.C. I called my cousin at her office and said I was going.

Before she left that morning, she'd already packed her things because she was heading to Charlotte, N.C., to meet my brother. After work, they planned to get in his car and drive to Raleigh, stay overnight with my aunt Mavis, then head to D.C.

My cousin said she'd come back for me, but I was still in pain. I knew the doctor couldn't be right when he said my elbows weren't injured. Every time I moved either elbow, I could hear fluid and blood sloshing about as if inside a balloon.

When my cousin came back to pick me up, I announced I would be driving to North Carolina. She replied, "You can't drive with a sling on!"

"Watch me," I replied defiantly.

On the highway, my cousin received a phone call I could overhear. What caught my attention was her saying that if anyone could make it, she could—that was odd phrasing. I had no idea the news I was about to receive.

An hour later, my cousin said, "Your grandmother is in the hospital."

"What for?"

"She couldn't receive her dialysis because the shunt in her arm wasn't working."

I didn't think much of it at first, as my grandmother had frequently been in and out of the hospital due to clogged shunts.

When we were about five minutes from my brother's house, my cousin said, "Your grandmother is in intensive care." She'd suffered a massive heart attack and was on life support.

"Why didn't you tell me sooner?"

"Because you were driving," she said.

"What does that have to do with anything?"

"If I had told you, you wouldn't have been able to handle the information, given how much you love your grandmother," she replied.

I was my grandmother's second-oldest grandchild, and everyone knew that when she fell ill, I wouldn't care where I was; I would be back in North Carolina within hours to support her.

Upon arriving at my brother's house, he looked stunned. He had just learned the news and shared my feelings for my grandmother; she raised us, and we were her favorites. We would do anything for her. If she had asked for one of my kidneys, I would have handed it over without hesitation.

My cousin and I moved our bags from her SUV into my brother's and said, "We're going to Greenville, N.C., to see our grandmother." It was a six-hour drive. In the bitter nine-degree cold, the temperature kept dropping. While en route, it seemed like everyone was texting each other—strange, but I couldn't connect the dots, as I was still aching and fatigued.

I thought I heard my cousin tell someone we were about three hours from the hospital, then she took a nap, and so did I. When we were about an hour from the hospital, my cousin started texting again, and the phone kept ringing. Concerned, I still had no idea what awaited me.

When we arrived at the hospital, my uncle met us at the entrance and said our grandmother was on the fifth floor. This particular hospital catered specifically to heart patients. He asked me how my elbows were doing.

"Like I always say when asked how I'm doing, I say fine," I replied.

Before heading upstairs to see my grandmother, my cousin mentioned she needed to use the restroom, so we waited for her. My brother, uncle, and I joked about how long she took—she had always been slow. When she finally emerged, my brother quipped, "You're just like an old lady; it always takes you forever to do anything."

My uncle kept mum about what awaited me inside my grandmother's room.

We got on the elevator and made our way to her room. I thought to myself, damn, there are a lot of people here. What kind of ICU is this, allowing so many visitors at once? I remained clueless about the reality I was about to face.

When I walked into the room, my mother and aunt Denderaunt greeted me, asking, "Gold, how's your arm?" I replied, "Fine." Gold is one of my many nicknames. I hugged a few people before quickly approaching my grandmother's bedside. She was breathing heavily, but a machine breathed for her. I grasped my grandmother's hand, saying, "What's up, Tess?"

My grandmother's name was Tessie.

"Open your eyes and get up," I urged. "Tess, your hands are cold. What's happening here?"

She took labored breaths. My grandmother's youngest daughter, Mavis, murmured, "Gold, she is gone."

"Gone where?"

"She's dead."

"How can she be dead?" I argued. "She's still breathing. She isn't dead until they pull the plug."

My aunt explained she had passed away about an hour prior; she had tried to hold on but couldn't. The first thought that flashed through my mind was that it made sense why my cousin's phone had been ringing continuously on our way—it was because she knew but chose not to let on.

After they cleaned my grandmother, I kissed her on the forehead and said goodbye. I was devastated. To this day, I struggle to cope with her loss. The rest of the family returned to our hometown, Kinston, North Carolina. My mind shifted, and I decided I wouldn't attend the inauguration. No disrespect to the president, but I was too hurt.

The next day, my brother and cousin went to D.C., but I refused to leave my grandmother until she was laid to rest. A couple of days before the funeral, I appeared on a local TV station for an interview concerning my first book. I called beforehand, intending to arrive when Obama was sworn in to lend context to the segment.

After showering, my mother gasped when she saw both my elbows. I thought to myself, what the hell is she screaming about?

"Gold, both of your elbows are black and blue! You must have broken several blood vessels when you fell," she exclaimed.

Me and the host agreed that I wouldn't do the show until I witnessed President Obama being sworn in as the 44th President.

On my way to the studio in the snow to promote the first version of my book "The True Character of a Man

I asked her to help me get dressed, and my sister drove me to the studio for the interview. Five inches of snow had fallen overnight. Following the funeral, my cousin, brother, and I returned to Charlotte to retrieve our vehicle and drive back to Atlanta. The next day, I visited my orthopedic physician, who informed me, "Both of your elbows are out of alignment." He could drain the fluid, but all the tendons in both elbows had been crushed, necessitating emergency surgery. He also needed to conduct an MRI for confirmation, but he had his assistant schedule the surgery for Friday.

"Let's do it Monday," I insisted, citing the Super Bowl on Sunday—I wanted to enjoy it without discomfort. Besides, the elbows had been compromised for almost two weeks. Another couple of days wouldn't hurt.

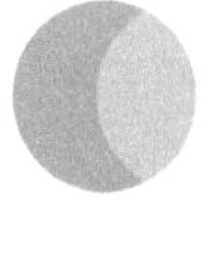

Reapplying for Social Security Benefits

After my Social Security benefits were denied for a second time, I continued to see my doctor and attend group therapy every Thursday. I was still taking my medication but wasn't feeling any better. I knew I had a lawsuit pending against the Social Security Administration, and it was going to take a long time to resolve.

One day, my doctor asked if I planned to apply for Social Security again. I replied no.

"Mr. Jones, you still can reapply for Social Security," my doctor insisted. But I told him every time I heard the words "Social Security," I felt sick. Of course, that was part of the Social Security Administration's strategy: to make you feel sick and tired so you give up and stop trying to claim your benefits. It's a damn shame when someone like me, who has worked all his life and paid into the system, gets denied when it comes time to receive benefits.

It's all one big political game to deny people their benefits, or to frustrate them to the point of either giving up or dying. I said to hell with Social Security—this is exactly how they want me to feel.

But my doctor pointed out something else. "Mr. Jones, we have a new president, and changes are being made. People are getting approved for Social Security within a year," he said.

I really didn't feel up to applying for the benefits again; my grandmother had just passed the month before, and I was dealing with two broken elbows. The stress was taking a considerable toll on me, both mentally and physically. I reluctantly reapplied for benefits in April 2009, and again in July 2009. Naturally, I was denied once more. I knew this would happen. I appealed the decision, but in October 2009, my appeal was denied.

Ninety-nine percent of the time, if you're not on dialysis or have cancer, you'll be denied immediately. After that final appeal, my paperwork went to the administrative law judge to set a hearing date for my case. I didn't have a representative at the time.

I decided to represent myself, but my doctor advised me to consider finding a representative when I got a hearing date. Vikki Hankins, vice president of my organization, handled all my paperwork from her home in Orlando. I didn't trust lawyers since they tend to rely on their clients to provide everything and still expect payment.

I wanted Vikki to represent me because she had put in the work and prepared all my briefs for two years for my Social

Security lawsuit. She was qualified and pursuing her paralegal degree. It isn't required to have a lawyer for your Social Security case, but you know as well as I do that courts often favor lawyers.

In November 2009, I attended my group session and shared my situation with my therapist. She knew someone who could help me and referred me to a representative who had successfully won several Social Security cases. Though not a lawyer, he held a Juris Doctor degree and was more than qualified to represent me; he wouldn't need to prepare because all the paperwork had been completed.

I thought to myself, if I win, I'll owe $6,000 to someone who didn't do half the work Vikki did—she worked her ass off for me. However, I promised myself I would compensate Vikki for her efforts on my behalf.

The first week in January 2010, I received a letter from the administrative law judge stating he had received my paperwork and would be in touch when we had a court date. I notified my representative, who told me to expect a court date in September. I expressed my impatience, declaring I would ask God to expedite the process.

Our church fasts on the third Wednesday of every month, and I remember my prayer: I'm tired of waiting for my Social Security case to come up in court. I asked God to expedite this case because I couldn't handle the stress of waiting any longer.

The following week was January 25, my birthday. I woke up that morning with plans. My first stop was church to praise and thank God for allowing me to see another year. I asked Him to expedite my Social Security hearing; it was time to conclude this process.

On February 1, I received a letter from the Administrative Law Judge informing me I had a hearing at 10 a.m. on April 6. The letter was dated January 25—the same day I asked God to expedite my hearing. I can't chalk that up to coincidence; I believe in the power of prayer and my faith in God, and He answered my request. All praise goes to Him.

I told my representative about the hearing date, and he almost had a heart attack. My good fortune shocked him, but not me; I know what God can do. The date of my hearing was one year and a week after I reapplied for benefits, so we didn't have much time to prepare, particularly since it caught my representative off guard, and my doctor takes his sweet time getting paperwork together for court.

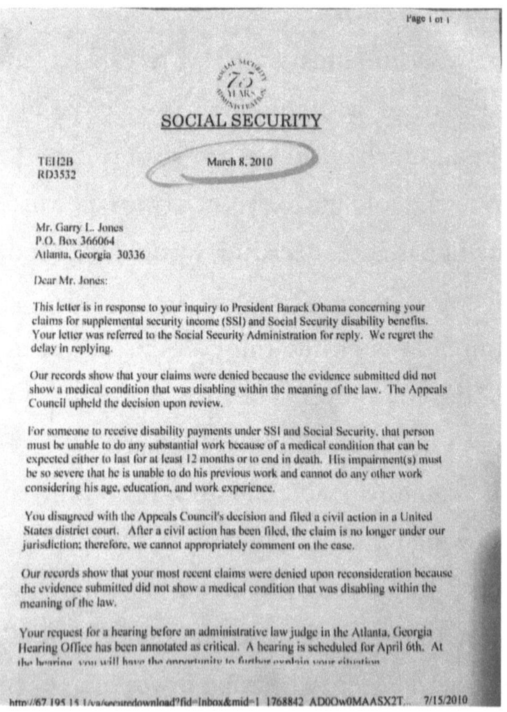

One of the letters about my Social Security Disability Benefits

The Show Down

I had six weeks before I faced another judge who would decide whether I was disabled. Most people think if you're disabled, you must be in a wheelchair, blind, mute, or unable to walk—but that's not true. Few acknowledge that depression, anxiety, and Post-Traumatic Stress Disorder are illnesses, but they are just as crippling as any other disease—possibly even worse. This affliction can rob you of sleep, lead you to overeat or undereat, and leave you feeling like you no longer want to live. A mental impairment, to me, is worse than a physical one.

For six weeks, I was in agony. I wanted that hearing over with. Every day dragged on like an eternity, as if the clock had stopped. I was painfully aware of the torment I suffered during the first round of my Social Security case, and I dreaded facing another rejection from the government. I came from a background of warriors, and I refused to give in; still, regardless of how strong you are mentally or physically, you can be broken. Warriors continue to rise and live to fight another day.

As my grandmother would say, "Garry, you have to press on." Somehow, I felt God was on my side, and with His support, who could be against me?

Yet I recognize that many can oppose you, regardless of your faith, simply because some are unconvinced by what God can do.

The week leading up to April 6, my heart sensed a showdown was imminent. I imagined the government thinking, we've thrown everything at Garry Jones, but he seems to have nine lives. Unknown to them, God won't allow you to die before fulfilling His mission—so if they can't kill me, a showdown is bound to arise. As my pastor, Aaron L. Parker from Zion Hill Baptist Church, explained in one of his Bible study lessons titled "Moving Toward Your Showdown," a showdown refers to an event, situation, or circumstance that necessitates resolving an issue. Although he wrote about this well after my Social Security case concluded, I now understand his meaning.

He often illustrated memorable showdowns in the Bible, including the confrontation between the prophet Elijah and the prophets at Queen Jezebel's table. As with most challenges, the two opposing sides featured one entity representing God and one manifesting as an enemy of the Lord. At a pivotal moment, God commands His representative to confront the opposition—indeed, to move toward a showdown. That decisive confrontation ultimately showcases God's superior power. The essence of his teaching was that as long as the Lord's representatives act according to God's commands, they—despite facing setbacks—will ultimately triumph over their rivals.

This parallel fits my situation perfectly on April 6, 2010.

My hearing was scheduled for 10:30 a.m. but didn't commence until 3:15 p.m. I had anticipated the wait, frustrations grew as I went to retrieve my phone from the car, only to find it had been booted. I had paid for an all-day pass, but the parking attendant was disinterested in hearing my case. Even with payment, there were areas in the lot where parking was prohibited; it was all very misleading.

I was furious, as I had to pay $75 to release my car. The anger seethed within me; I could have throttled the booting agent, who was irritatingly dismissive of my valid receipt. My representative had to venture outside the courthouse to help calm me down. That was how built-up my stress had become over the past six weeks. I was at a boiling point, desperate to lash out at someone.

When I finally met the judge, I was ready for a fight, but the hearing lasted a mere two minutes. He reviewed my case and ruled in my favor. He inquired whether I had health insurance and promised to expedite my case.

He did mention one peculiar detail: my case had been "everywhere." The government listed my file as a fraud case, but after I wrote to the president and he inquired about it, the gears likely moved a little faster because I refused to go down without a fight.

The judge did inform me he couldn't grant back pay because the Social Security Administration insisted I didn't become disabled until February 2008. How in the hell did they pinpoint that date? I had to medically retire from my job in 2003, yet someone in the administration claimed I didn't become disabled until 2008.

Rest assured, I'm not done with Social Security—they owe me back pay all the way back to 2003. They cheated me out of five years. They continue to play games, but it's time for their charades to end, given that I just wrote to the president again, seeking clarity on how Social Security derived that conclusion. The injustices I've witnessed throughout my life are what compelled me to become Advocate4Justice.

As long as I live, if there is no justice, there will be no peace.

REFERENCES

1. Hightower, J. (n.d.). The Next Best Thing to Slaves. Retrieved from Flat Rock website: http://flatrock.org.nz/topics/prisons/made_in_the_usa.htm

2. Schwartzapfel, B. (2009). Your Valentine, Made in Prison. Retrieved from Prison Legal News website: https://www.prisonlegalnews.org/displayNews.aspx?newsid=216&AspxAutoDetectCookieSupport=1

3. Shachtman, N. (2011). Prisoners Help Build Patriot Missiles. Retrieved from Wired website: http://www.wired.com/dangerroom/2011/03/prisoners-help-build-patriot-missiles/

4. U.S. Department of Justice. Work in American Prisons: Joint Ventures with the Private Sector. Retrieved from National Institute of Justice Program Focus website: https://www.ncjrs.gov/pdffiles/workampr.pdf